TBI HELL
A TRAUMATIC
BRAIN INJURY
REALLY SUCKS

GEO GOSLING

Outskirts Press, Inc.
Denver, Colorado

TBI Hell
A Traumatic Brain Injury really sucks
All Rights Reserved
Copyright © 2006 Geo Gosling
VR1.1

Outskirts Press
http://www.outskirtspress.com

ISBN-10: -1-59800-722-X
ISBN-13: 978-1-59800-722-0

Outskirts Press and the "OP" logo are trademarks belonging to Outskirts Press, Inc.

Printed in the United States of America

TBI HELL

CHAPTER 1

"Shut up and get me some fuckin' water!" Those were my first words and the first thing I remember upon awakening. My sister was just droning on and on about stuff that I had absolutely no interest in, and I was tired and just wanted to sleep. So, me being me, just told her to shut up. I had no idea what my sister was doing near me in bed. Plus, I was thirsty and couldn't get up for a drink. My other sisters, yes there were more than one, and my mom were there also, and they were all elated that I had spoken. That was my first clue that something was amiss, because normally I won't shut up. A young adult woman then came in to the room; when told what I had said, she seemed genuinely happy. Shortly thereafter an adult male was told of my utterances and he seemed relieved. I thought, *What the hell is going on?* I couldn't understand why everyone was so happy about what I had said. Speaking of everyone, who were all these people? What was my Mom doing here, and why didn't she frown upon me for using the "f" word? What were all my sisters doing here?

I don't really know what happened next or how much time elapsed before it happened. I just remember lying in bed and hearing my brother-in-law tell me I was in a bike (bicycle) accident. I thought, *Gee, must have been a doozy.* I didn't quite get the gravity of the situation. I didn't even realize where I was.

I must have crashed my mountain bike. I'm pretty good at doing silly stuff on that bike. I figured I had jumped off something or hit something and broken a few bones, it couldn't

1

be worse than that. Boy, was I wrong! The reason I thought that, was because I consider myself a competent and capable rider. I had been riding bikes since I was little kid. I rode my Western Flyer everywhere, all the time. As I grew older and more mature (no laughing) I replaced my beat-up ol' Western Flyer with a twenty-four-speed mountain bike. Now I could ride faster, jump higher, and just generally do more testosterone-induced silly stuff.

I had recently discovered NORBA (National Off Road Bicycle Association) and racing mountain bikes. I loved it! Like everything else I enjoy, I dove into it full bore. I raced in NORBA as a beginner until I had won enough races to qualify to race for the Sport class (the next class after being a beginner). Having made it to this class in a relatively short period of time, I was getting cocky.

The season for mountain-bike racing is only a few months a year. I couldn't get enough of going fast on my bike and I wanted to get a lot better at racing, so I decided to ride-year round. I lived in the Napa Valley where you needed to drive in order to get to some good biking trails. Putting my bike on the car, getting all my stuff together, driving to and from the trails, and wallowing in the mud got old after a while. I then decided I could at least stay in good physical riding shape if I rode my road bicycle, during the fall and winter. So I did...a lot.

I started doing criteriums (a short, fast, multiple-lap race around a short course) in Santa Rosa one night a week during the summer. In order to win criteriums, or crits, you need to ride fast. So, logically, I decided I needed to practice riding fast...all the time. Uphill, downhill, flatlands, mud, pavement, it didn't matter to me; I just wanted to go fast. Maybe it's just some male thing, I don't really know.

One warm, beautiful day in the wine country (I lived in St. Helena, California) I decided to ride my road bicycle, a Bianchi, up to Angwin and back. My parents live in Angwin and I was raised there. Angwin is located at 1667 ft. on top of Howell Mountain, which helps form the eastern side of the

Napa Valley. About halfway to the top, I looked ahead and saw what just about every unattached biker dreams of; some long, tan, smooth, well-toned legs, attached to a woman. Well, I managed to ride even faster! I caught up with her, and since she was not wearing a helmet, I had a good excuse to talk with her and tell her she should be wearing one.

It turned out that the girl's father was my science teacher in junior high school. I rode with her all the way to her house, talking all the way, and talked with her some more once we got there.

In the right situations, I could talk for hours. Once, while in high school, two of my friends and I went skiing at Squaw Valley. The parking lot, highway, and everything else was totally packed, it was pretty slow going. It took us about three hours to get back to St. Helena. I told jokes the entire way home. As soon as I would start a joke, I would remember another, and so on. My two friends probably said only twenty words for the entire trip home. I don't talk much anymore.

Anyway, I became friends with this girl, whose name was Cerise. At the time, I was twenty-five years old and I think she was only nineteen. I grew up with three older sisters and one twin sister, and one thing I learned is that one doesn't come out and ask a woman her age. It's a "no win" situation.

Cerise expressed an interest in bicycle riding and wanted to take it up. She didn't want to race, just ride for enjoyment and exercise. That sounds oxymoronic but when it comes to bicycle riding, it isn't. I, of course, was more than happy to help in any way possible. The first bit of advice I gave her was to get a bicycle helmet.

I had agreed to go on a ride with her after I got off work on September 15, 1995. I got off work around 4:00 P.M. I went home, changed into my biking clothes, jumped on my bike, and rode up to Cerise's house. We went on a ride until just about dusk. The day was a Friday. Angwin is a Seventh Day Adventist Community and church is a very important to them. Their Sabbath is from sundown Friday to sundown Saturday. I am not an Adventist, but Cerise and her family are devout Adventists and recognizing the Sabbath is important to them. We returned from our ride that Friday and Cerise wanted to go to Vespers, (which is a Seventh Day Adventist meeting). She did, however, offer to give me a ride home, as the sun was sinking fast and it was becoming bicycle unfriendly.

Trying to be a stud and impress the girl, I declined and said I'd ride home. I should mention now, that for reasons the reader will discern later, I don't remember any of this. I'm just guessing based on what I've been told and what I know of myself.

Off I went. I was tired from working all day and going for a bicycle ride. I had a girl and religion on my mind. Needless to say, I wasn't thinking too clearly. I should also mention that the bicycle I was riding was a Bianchi, which is made in Italy for racing. It had no parts, and therefore no weight, that wasn't absolutely necessary for racing. As a result, it was fast and didn't have any lawsuit-induced safety equipment attached (i.e., reflectors). I didn't have any sort of light either.

I was coming down from 1600 feet, hungry, horny, and tired. I was thinking of things besides riding a bicycle. I was going as fast as I possibly could, because I wanted to get home before it got totally dark.

On the way down there is a stop sign at the top of a very steep section of hill. It is only a three-way stop and all the roads are very visible. Chances are I didn't even slow down, let alone stop, because I was in a hurry and no one was coming. I kept right on going and went down the steepest section of the hill. At the bottom there is a road, Crystal Springs, which adjoins the road I was on. Crystal Springs adjoins to my right as I went downhill.

As luck would have it, a person was driving up the road as I was going down. The driver turned left onto Crystal Springs. The speed limit on that hill is 35 MPH. It is estimated I was going between 40-50 MPH. It doesn't take a vivid imagination to figure out what happened next.

The driver didn't see me, obviously. It was 7:55 p.m and I

didn't have a bike light or reflectors. Now, everyone automatically assumes that is why I wasn't seen. I, being the stubborn, macho guy that I am, have different ideas. The main problem for me is I don't remember a thing. I know what I *think* must have happened, based on the decisions I normally make when encountering a vehicle.

There are three items that I consider very important in explaining what took place and, of course, absolving myself of any guilt for what happened to me. Number 1: the driver of the car had a newborn infant with her. The driver, mother of the baby, most likely had a great deal of focus on the child, and not so much on the road. I don't fault her at all for that; it's probably a natural instinct that the mother in any and all species has. She probably heard the kid sneeze or something, just took a quick glance up the road, didn't see anything or anyone, looked at the kid, and turned left. That brings me to number 2: the streetlight wasn't working (I think). Had it been working, thus illuminating the area I was riding in, I might have been seen. Notice I used the word "might." As I said before, I didn't have any reflectors, which I should have. To make a long story short: she didn't see me, I was breaking the speed limit, she turned left, and I hit her. Number 3: I believe the driver was not using her directional signal. I have absolutely no proof of this. I do, however, know how I would ride when encountering a vehicle with its signal light on. First, I wouldn't necessarily slow down, but I would proceed with caution. I would think of "escape routes" in case the vehicle did turn in front of me. I would position my body, hands, and arms so I could immediately hit the brakes if need be. I would consider a total plan of action to avoid colliding with the vehicle. As the car and I approached each other, I would look at the driver to see if I could discern his intention, hoping he had seen me and intended to turn after I went by. I would always think, *Okay...If he turns now, I'll do this...Okay...now I'll do this.* As the vehicle and I got close enough that I didn't have an "escape route," I would think, *Okay...if he turns now,*

I'm fucked!

If an oncoming vehicle did not have its directional on, I wouldn't assume it was turning but intended to continue going straight. This is why I am fairly certain the driver did not signal before she turned. Again, I have no proof of this, and since I had just come from a ride with a girl I was interested in, there's no telling what the hell I was thinking.

CHAPTER 2

So here I am, twenty-five years old, just been riding bicycles with a babe, looking forward to the weekend, having a job I really enjoy, and basically just enjoying life.

It was 7:55 p.m., so there wasn't much sunlight left. I, of course, was riding like a bat out of hell. A 1950 yellow pick up truck (with an infant that was only a week or two old) was coming up the hill. Again, I didn't have any reflectors or even a bike light. The truck turned left onto Crystal Springs and I tried to break one of the basic laws of physics. The law that says two pieces of matter cannot occupy the same space at the same time, or something like that. Well, I certainly proved that law. I hit the truck, and ended up on the side of the road all bloody and unconscious. The driver of the truck, who'll remain nameless, freaked out and started screaming. People at a nearby house heard her and called an ambulance. The collision happened only half of a mile from The St. Helena Hospital and Health Center (S.H.H.C). I was not taken there, however. I was routed to The Queen of the Valley Hospital in Napa, located 20 -30 minutes away. I was routed to Napa because The Queen has a much better equipped and staffed trauma unit.

Having survived this accident, I had amongst many other injuries, a TBI, or Traumatic Brain Injury. If you ask me, that is a pretty redundant name. What the hell would an Un-traumatic Brain Injury be? I also had a broken neck. I fractured the C6, C7, and C8 vertebrae. Those are at the base of the neck. My right shoulder was also pretty much destroyed. There are a number of reasons why I didn't die. I'll share with the reader the main reasons that I believe I am still alive.

The first, and probably most important, is that I was wearing a bicycle helmet. The helmet is now split on one side, cracked in other places, and is shaved down on the right, front side. If my skull had received only a fraction of the damage my helmet did, I wouldn't be alive, or I'd be a vegetable, at best. The second is my right shoulder. It bore the brunt of the collision with the truck. Had my shoulder not done so, I don't believe the helmet could have saved me. The next reason is all the people in the medical field. The emergency medical technicians (EMTs), who were the first to treat me, kept me alive long enough to get to the hospital. Another reason is the woman who made the decision to route the ambulance to The Queen of the Valley hospital rather than S.H.H.H.C. because The Queen is much better prepared for head trauma. The final reason: I was in extremely good physical condition. I had very little fat on my body and my heart was in excellent shape, from all the riding I'd been doing. So riding my bicycle nearly got me killed but I believe it also helped save me.

Back to the helmet. As I said, the helmet was cracked, split, and shaved down on the right, front side. I don't how it got that way. I can only speculate. I believe my helmet was shaved down because my head must have slid along the pavement after I collided with the truck. The helmet, sliding along the asphalt, created enough friction to tear through the plastic cover and then shave down the material that composes the helmet. I don't even want to think what might have happened to my head had I not being wearing a helmet. It doesn't take a genius to figure out I would not be alive today. I can't stress enough the importance of wearing a helmet.

Now, I must admit, I never wore a helmet as a kid riding my Western Flyer around the yard. I very rarely rode on pavement as a kid, and trees don't turn left in front of you. As a youngster I, nor anyone else, was very aware of head trauma. I also never wore one during the five years I spent at the

University of California, Davis (UCD). I probably should have, but UCD and the town of Davis, California, are set up for bicyclists, and the people in the town are very accustomed to us riding all over. So they are used to looking for and seeing cyclists. This results in relatively safe riding conditions. In retrospect, I probably should have been wearing a helmet during my time at UCD because the bicycle rider rides on the same streets with cars, buses, big trucks, etc. Hindsight is 20/20 and I came through fine, so I don't think about it too often. Back to hitting the truck.

An ambulance picked me up and drove to Queen of the Valley Hospital. Incidentally, I learned after being released from the hospital that one of the EMT's knew me but I was so covered in blood he didn't recognize me until later. Apparently, I hit the truck and flew over it. Unfortunately, my upper thigh caught on some part of the truck and, as I flew over, a big gash was ripped in it. I think that must be where most of the blood came from. I came to rest on the on the upward-sloped bank on the opposite side of the road. People in a nearby house were having a barbecue or something, and heard the woman who had been driving the truck screaming or crying. Someone there was the person who called for an ambulance.

Geo Gosling wearing the helmet that saved his life.

CHAPTER 3

Now it gets sketchy. As I mentioned earlier, I told my sister to get me some water. That is my first memory and it came after I'd been in Intensive Care for two weeks.

Fortunately, I guess, I was never technically in a coma. The neurosurgeon, Dr. Vince Morgesi, illustrated this to my parents by bringing them to my room, or wherever I was, and then yelling at me. I would just lie there and give him the finger, flip him off. If I had been in a coma I wouldn't have responded at all. I was just unconscious for about a week.

I do remember being in a room with someone else for, I think, just one night. Then I was either moved or the other patient left, I'm not sure which, but I had a room to myself. At some point during all this I was out in a hallway with a portable TV and VCR. A friend of mine, from college, had given me three videotapes of Metallica in concert. I'm a big fan and so I really wanted to watch the videotapes. So I did. Picture this: I'm sitting in the hallway, outside my room, at a busy hospital. I've got a portable TV-VCR combo set up and I'm playing a Metallica concert. If you're not familiar with Metallica, they are a hard rock, a.k.a. heavy metal, band. They play loud, obnoxious, fast, and they cuss a lot. I loved it! During my viewing nurses, doctors, and elderly volunteers walked by. The looks I got were priceless. I loved that even more!

My doctors, nurses, and various therapists wanted me to go into the hospital's acute rehabilitation unit. However, my insurance company, which shall remain nameless, didn't want to pay for it and instead wanted to put me in a nursing home. I'm guessing that the insurance company thought I would be a vegetable and didn't want to pay all the hospital bills. My doctor, Dr. Marco Bodor, my nurses, and my various therapists all went to bat for me. They told the insurance company that I was making good progress and could, with proper care be pretty "normal."   Fortunately, they convinced the insurance company that Acute Rehab was the best option for me. So, my doctor, nurses, therapists hit a grand slam in the bottom of the ninth for me.

Now I will get on a soap box. Why in the hell can an insurance company make medical decisions that will totally affect a person's entire life? I've heard of quite a few other cases like mine, so mine was not an isolated one. I realize we live in a capitalist society, and that's fine, but that was ridiculous. I can't believe we have gotten to the point where insurance companies, to save a few bucks, can tell people in the medical profession what they should do with a patient. That, is just totally, absolutely, fucking wrong!

All those who went to bat for me probably saved my life. If I had to live in a nursing home with people who weren't able to take care of themselves, I would have found a way to kill myself. As it was, I had to go back home and live with my parents because I wasn't even able to brush my teeth. I couldn't bathe or shower, I couldn't completely dress myself, and I couldn't prepare meals, not that I could really do that before the accident.

CHAPTER 4

So I was moved from acute care, which is where I was after Intensive Care, to acute rehabilitation. This is where you get a cute therapist to help you get well. Well, just kidding. Acute Rehab is where all you do is physical, mental, and occupational therapy to help you get well. In my case, however, Acute Rehab did include a cute therapist. There were actually three or four really cute therapists. I don't know what the Chinese Water Torture is, obviously, but I do know what the TBI torture is. It's being a recent college graduate, single, surrounded by young cute women, and being in no shape to impress them. I wear contact lenses and they were taken out somewhere along the line and I couldn't put them back in. So I had to wear my glasses. I couldn't shave or comb my hair. I couldn't bathe or shower on my own so I would get pretty ripe. But worst of all by far, was the fact that I couldn't wipe my rear end after doing my business. Not only does that make it hard to impress chics, but it just messes with your own head. Here you are, a college graduate, very physically fit, single, getting to the age where you're tired of drinking beer, and now you have to be wiped after taking a crap. I don't know the proper psychological term for how I felt; all I know is that it was totally embarrassing! Wait, it gets worse.

Before I proceed, I must say this not meant to be derogatory in any way. It is not meant to show lack of respect or anything like that. I have four sisters, for heaven's sake! So, here goes. The worst, most embarrassing, most disturbing, most depressing thing was that I had sit down on the toilet to pee. Maybe it's just a macho guy thing, but it really disturbed me! Now, this was after I had progressed past the need to use the catheter and wear diapers.

About the catheter. Once you get past the initial fear and embarrassment, a catheter is pretty cool. A nurse comes, slips a tube into your penis and into your bladder, and your bladder empties. You don't even have to push! You just lie there and watch TV.

Why did I think a catheter was the best thing going? I'll tell you. I would have to go pee a couple of times per day. It would be a total ordeal. Let me explain.

First, I would have to locate and then grab and push the "nurse call-button."

Second, I would have wait for someone to come, which, occasionally, took what felt like an eternity

Third, I would have to be helped out of bed and into a wheelchair.

Fourth, I would have to be helped out of the wheelchair and onto the toilet.

Fifth, I would sit on the toilet and pee, a step that's a lot harder than it sounds.

Now, all this was after I had sufficiently recovered to be able to get out of bed in order to pee. Prior to this, I had to pee in bed, in a little hand-held urinal or "jug" as I called it. If I had to pee, I would just grab the jug, drop my drawers, and pee in the jug. Sound simple? Trust me, it wasn't. I would lay in bed, my penis in the jug, watching TV, for what seemed like hours. Eventually, my bladder would be empty enough so that I could get my mind off the fact that I had to pee. I don't think I ever got my bladder completely empty using the jug. That's what the catheter was for. I did, however, have to be helped out of bed once a day to take a bowel movement (B.M.).

After I took a B.M., I would have to be wiped, because I couldn't do it myself. I'm not sure why I couldn't; I just know I couldn't. Next to the toilet was a switch for a buzzer to alert a nurse. I would press the switch and wait. A nurse would come and wipe me and, of course, make observations about my B.M.

I would hear if it was large or small, soft or hard, dark or light. There are some things a person is not meant to know.

If you have been around mothers with newborns, the B.M. is a popular topic. The mothers talk about the frequency, color, consistency, and even the odor of their newborns' bowel movements. I don't know about the odor, but I heard everything else about my B.M. I was basically a newborn and so my "mothers," the nurses, would discuss my B.M.s. If I didn't go once every day, I would get a suppository that night. This was all very disturbing to me. Anyway, back to step five in the "pee ordeal."

I would know I had to pee, badly. As my mother would say, "I had to pee so bad, I could taste it." I'm sure at some point in your life you had to pee very badly, but had nowhere to go, or couldn't get away from some responsibility. As the minutes ticked by you had to go worse and worse. It would almost become painful. This was the feeling I had constantly, every day. I would lie in my hospital bed, watching TV or trying to sleep, and the only thing I could think about was how badly I had to pee. I would have to pee so badly, it would hurt. Problem was, I just physically and/or mentally, couldn't go. I would go through the whole ordeal described above, but I just couldn't empty my bladder. I would ask the nurse to turn the water on in the sink. I was hoping the running water would, psychologically, do something to help me pee. I don't know if it did or not, but at least I felt I was doing something to help the situation. I'm sure there is some medical condition having to do with brain injuries to explain why had trouble "relieving" myself, but I have my own theory. Now, before I give my own theory, I don't mean to offend any females. As I said, I have four sisters, and I never got away with saying anything even remotely offensive or derogatory towards women. That said, here is my "theory."

I believe I couldn't pee partly because of my brain injury but also, and more importantly, because it was psychologically such a blow to my manhood. If you have to pee really badly, and you are a guy, you just find a tree or bush to hide behind, unzip your pants, and go for it.

If you are a woman, you still have to find a tree, or bush, or something to hide behind. In addition, however, the spot has to allow you to squat down, has to allow your urine to dissipate without leaving any noticeable trace on any article of your clothing, and, ideally you should have something to wipe your body clean. The fact that I had to sit down to urinate was just too much for me to deal with. That was step 5.

Sixth, I would have to push a button near the toilet to call the nurse back to the bathroom and wait for her, or him, to come.

Seventh, I would have to be pushed back into my room and helped back into bed.

Now, I had made enough progress in my recovery that I could use the toilet and didn't require a catheter, but a catheter was a hell of a lot easier, both mentally and physically, than using the toilet.

One trip to the bathroom and I was worn out for a few hours; I would need a nap. Now, it becomes apparent why I thought the catheter was so great.

I won't say much about the diapers I had to wear because I don't remember much about them. They were the Depends Undergarments that you see advertised for senior citizens. I think I wore them all the time, just in case. I didn't have much control over the "removal" thing. It was such an arduous task to do the removal thing that I tried to do it as little as possible.

Believe it or not, it was comforting to be wearing diapers. I knew it was really hard to go to bathroom, so I figured if I had to relieve myself, and was actually able to do so, I would just do it.

It was rather disturbing to be wearing diapers, but it was a good source of amusement. I, along with family and friends, never got tired of making wisecracks. Most of them involved Pampers or Huggies. The best ones, however, involved those pull-up things that kids on the verge of being potty-trained wear, and on the TV commercial sing, "...look at me! I'm a big kid now!"

CHAPTER 5

I had to go to the bathroom because I ate. I couldn't eat "normally" at first, mainly because I couldn't swallow. I had "food" put into me with an IV. I put "food" in quotes because it was just some liquid that contained all the necessary calories, vitamins, minerals, etc. that the body needs to survive. I also had a tracheotomy so that I could breath. A tracheotomy is a hole cut in the base of your neck with a tube inserted. I've been told that one day I just ripped out the tube and threw it down. I have no idea why I would do such a thing. My mother happened to be there at the time, and she freaked out. Apparently, I came out okay.

Eventually I came to the point where I could swallow, thus using my mouth for its intended purpose. I couldn't however, feed myself. I had to have someone feed me. Talk about embarrassing! Plus, I was wearing diapers. I was a newborn, again. I felt like the guy who had a bachelor of science degree, was an assistant wine maker/cellarmaster, and raced bicycles, was dead. In his place was a little baby who couldn't feed himself and had to wear diapers. More similarities to a little baby will come up later.

I could eat, but I needed help getting the food into my mouth. My oldest sister came often to feed me in the morning on her way to work. Other family members or a member of the hospital staff would feed me the other meals. They would bring the spoon or fork up to my mouth, I would open my mouth, and the food would go in. I would again feel like a little baby. I kept waiting to hear, "Here comes the airplane! There's the hanger! Open the hanger! Good! Now the plane lands and goes in the hanger!" That's what a lot of adults do to try to get their kids to eat. Every time I ate it was like giving my ego a good swift kick in the crotch! Talk about depressing.

Eventually, I don't know how long it took, I was able to feed myself. That was good, but talk about an arduous task! It would require me so much effort to feed myself, that I would be hungrier after I ate than I was before I started. Well no, not really, but it sure seemed like it.

I'm right handed but my right shoulder was pretty much useless. It was pretty much useless because my right deltoid muscle didn't work to well. It didn't work so well because in my crash the nerve to my deltoid muscle was stretched. Not broken or torn, but stretched. Therefore, it would heal as good as new, eventually. At least that's what the doctor told me. I was told it would take approximately 200 days. On the door to my hospital room I had a large calendar. I wrote a 200 on the day I was told this. Each successive day I would write the previous day's number minus one. I did this to give me something to do. Back to feeding myself.

Since my right deltoid muscle was pretty much shot, I tried eating with only my left hand. It's harder than it sounds. I got really good at making messes, both on myself and on the table and floor. I also made a mess of one of the therapists one day. I don't really remember how or why this happened, but I do remember it. I had coffee every morning, and on this particular morning, one of the cute therapists was helping me eat. I just remember unintentionally throwing the entire contents of my coffee cup all over the therapist. She was fine, because the coffee wasn't that hot, but she did have to go home and change.

The therapist, named Caroline, was about my age, and darn cute. Apparently, I nicknamed her "Honeydew chic." I don't ever remember calling her that, but my family says I did. They also asked me why I called her that. I didn't have a clue. After I had gotten out the hospital and moved back home, it occurred to me why I had nicknamed her "honeydew chic." A honeydew is a relatively large melon, and Caroline had nice "melons." At least I think that was the reason. Anyway, I got tired of making messes with my left hand so I used my right hand. I would lean forward, with my mouth a few inches above my plate, and just shovel food in. I would make a pretty good mess. Martha Stewart would have had a heart attack had she been present.

Once I had food in my mouth, I would chew and then swallow. Sounds simple enough, but it took a great effort to chew and swallow. In addition, I was really good at biting down hard on my tongue. The pain was excruciating! Pain tends to tire the body out, so after I was done biting my tongue, and eating, I would need a nap.

I am not a doctor or neurologist, but I do have my own explanation for my propensity to bite my tongue. I think that because of my brain injury, my brain just didn't really know where my tongue was at a given time. All my brain could handle at the time was getting the food into my mouth, and then having my mouth chew the food, and then swallowing. Knowing the actual location of my tongue was just sort of a nuisance for my brain, so it focused on the most important thing: eating the food. This tongue biting continued after I had gotten out of the hospital and moved in with my parents. It became less frequent, and now I haven't bit my tongue for a couple of years. It's nice to be able to eat a meal without any incidents of excruciating pain.

There was something else about meal times that are out of the ordinary. I ate alone; well there were no other patients, just a family member or a member of the hospital staff to help me shovel food into my mouth. I don't really know when or why I was allowed to eat alone, I just know I was happier that way. I sort of remember why I was allowed to do so. I ate with other patients at first and I remember I didn't like it. The other patients were all older, they could talk and relate to each other, and I had nothing in common with them. There was another reason I didn't like eating with other people, which I will explain.

CHAPTER 6

The other reason I didn't like to eat with the other patients is that it was really depressing. It had to do with the fact that they would all be talking and I couldn't really talk. I was a little baby, remember? One of the results of the head injury was that I couldn't regulate the speed of my speech. It was as if my tongue and mouth just couldn't keep up with what my brain was thinking. Wanting to say something, in response to what other patients were saying, I would think of what to say and then try to say it. However, my tongue just wouldn't do what it should have and what I wanted to say just came out as unintelligible noise. If I really concentrated on speaking s-l-o-w-l-y, I could be easily understood, but it took so much concentration and effort that I just said, "The hell with it!" So, being able to eat alone was a good thing.

I now have another problem in my mouth: both the upper and lower gums on the left side hurt like hell. They've been hurting for years and there is no end in sight. I've talked with Dr. Bodor, who called my dentist and told him to try something on me.

The dentist put quite a bit of whatever he uses to numb patients gums, on my gums. He then numbed my cheeks, lips, and everything else near there. Now, if the pain in my gums decreased or went away entirely, then that would indicate there was a problem in my gums. If not, that would indicate a different problem altogether. Dr. Bodor explained it to me, but it was beyond my comprehension. It had to do with a major nerve going to my brain, that it wasn't my gums that actually hurt; my brain just thought they did.

I'll tell you what I think about it. It's pretty well known that the right side of your brain controls the left side of your body and vice-versa. I hit the pickup truck with the right side of my head, therefore, the right side of my brain. I believe that the part of my brain that is responsible for monitoring my gums was injured. Some nerve was telling the right side of my brain that something was amiss, but since the nerve was injured and was telling an injured brain that something was wrong, the message got misinterpreted: the gums on the left side hurt.

I've seen another doctor in San Francisco, who specializes in the gums, and he saw nothing wrong with my gums. He thought maybe I should try flossing my teeth more often, which I did. I had been wearing a bite plate at night because it was thought maybe my gums hurt from clenching my teeth really hard at night. This doctor looked at my bite plate and thought it looked fine. He gave a couple other suggestions that were pretty out-there. He said I should eat seaweed to help improve my blood flow because that would help my gums. He said I should remove the earring in my left ear because I was "out of balance" with it in. I tried both of these suggestions because I was desperate and willing to try anything. My gums still hurt really bad. I don't think I can describe how annoying and frustrating it is to have pain in your gums twenty-four hours a day, seven days a week. Anyway, back to a cute nurse in acute rehab.

CHAPTER 7

I did more in acute rehab than eat and pee. One of the first things I did was learn how to write again, because I had forgotten how. The first time I tried to write it just came out as a bunch of scribbles. I don't remember actually being taught to write again, but there is one lesson, or assignment, that I do remember.

It was the first writing assignment the therapist had me do. It was to write, and sign, a check. Looking back on that, I think that is pretty darn amusing. The hospital knows you will be paying them for years to come, so they make sure you can write them a check. I, like most other Americans, had written numerous checks in my life. When I was given a check I knew what it was and its purpose. I thought, *No problem. I can write a check,* but when the therapist asked me to fill it out, I had no clue what to do. The more I thought about it, the more frustrated and angry I got. I would think *It's a fucking check! You've written a lot of those! You know what to do, so do it!* Problem was, I couldn't do it. I couldn't remember where the numbers went, where the date went, where the name of whomever I was writing the check to went. It was maddening! There was one activity later on that made this pale in comparison, but I'll get to that due time.

Eventually, I got the check written with some good coaching. I don't remember how legible my writing was, but I guess the hospital's bank would have been able to cash it.

When I went back to my room after all this, I had to sort of chuckle. I felt like I was living in dog years. I guess a dog ages seven years for every one-year that humans age. Well here I was, having just been born a few weeks ago. I was already eating solid foods, was being potty trained, could write legibly, and was being taught to write checks. I was living in TBI years. Every day in a TBI year is equivalent to about five regular human years.

Now comes the most frustrating thing. The episode where it hit me that things were definitely wrong. A later episode really opened my eyes to the fact that my life was all screwed up, but that's for later.

My therapist, Honeydew Chic, brought out a board with two shoelaces attached. I was going to learn how to tie my own shoes. At first I thought, *You've got to be kidding. Tie my own shoes? Gee, I've never done that before.* I wonder how many times the average adult has tied their shoe. I wasn't sure she was serious. Of course I can tie my own shoes. Well, I was wrong, again. I had the "shoe" on the table in front of me; I grabbed the laces, picked them up, and thought, *Hmmm. Now what?* I couldn't remember, for the life of me, how to tie a shoe. The more I thought about it, the more upset I got. I would think, *Damnit! You are a grown man. You have a Bachelor of Science degree from the University of California. You are the cellarmaster/asst. wine maker at a premium winery. You are a pretty intelligent dude, so why the fuck can't you tie a shoe?* Honeydew chic saw I was becoming visibly agitated, so she helped me tie the "shoe." I don't think I'll ever forget that experience. It was just ...so...weird. I was wheeled back to my room, because I couldn't walk, and helped into bed. As I lay in bed I started to realize something was seriously wrong. I didn't really realize how wrong things were, but there was something definitely wrong. I couldn't even tie my shoe in front of a cute girl! This was not the episode that caused me to realize my life was totally changed, or that caused severe depression. It just sort of made me realize that I had, in fact, injured my head somehow and things would be different.

I should mention here just what a total tiring ordeal it was just to get in and out of bed. I couldn't really get in and/or out of bed on my own. I would have to get help to get into position to get out of bed. Then I would require help to actually get out of bed. I would have to have help to then get into a wheelchair, and then pushed wherever I was to go. Getting back into bed was just a reverse of getting out of bed. Except it was harder because I was going up into the bed instead of down into a wheelchair. Getting into and out of bed was a hell of a workout.

Once in bed, I was to worn-out to do much. I slept...a lot. I also watched way too much TV. Before my accident I lived by myself in a studio apartment. I didn't own a TV. I had a stereo and listened to music a lot. Plus, I wasn't home much. I was either working, riding a bicycle, or something else outdoors. I played a lot of roller hockey, I played a little golf, I played my guitar, or I climbed rocks. I had no interest in TV. If I really wanted to watch the 49ers play football or the Giants play baseball, I would go to my parent's house and watch the game there.

In the hospital, however, I thought TV was great. I could lie in bed and watch TV for hours. I didn't have a whole hell of a lot of choice of things to do. I couldn't get out of bed on my own and I couldn't walk, yet. I loved watching those talk shows like Rikki Lake, Jenny Jones, or Jerry Springer. Now, the reason I liked watching them may surprise you. I found them to be uplifting. I could watch the shows and think, *I don't care how screwed up my life is now, at least I'm not that guy. He's got real problems! Man is he screwed-up!* However, after watching those shows for a few weeks, they became pretty depressing. I would think, *Man they are screwed up, but at least they are not stuck in a hospital. They can get out of bed and walk around without having to call and wait for someone to help them. Their lives may be crappy, but it's better than what is left of my life.*

Talking about watching TV reminds me of a funny story. I

said before there were a lot of older patients in acute rehab. Some were hard of hearing. One gentleman in the room next to me was especially hard of hearing. He would have the TV turned up so loud I could hear it in my room, over the sound of my own television. I would get a headache from listening to two separate programs at once. Well, if you can't beat 'em, join 'em. I would just tune my television to the program he was watching, put my television on "mute" and just listen to his. Problem solved, headaches gone.

I also liked watching sports, still do. On Sunday my Dad would come down and sit in my room, and we would watch the 49er game. I thought that was pretty cool. However, I like playing sports much better than watching them on TV. It was nice having my dad there to watch games with, but I would actually get incredibly antsy. Problem was, I couldn't do a damn thing about it. I couldn't get out of bed, I couldn't walk, I couldn't really do much except get pissed-off and frustrated, which, of course, I did. I still am.

CHAPTER 8

I didn't just eat, pee, and get pissed-off in acute rehab. I did a lot of work. The biggest "job" I had was re-learning to walk. Before that, however, my body had to do some healing.

As I stated earlier, I had a broken neck. Now I, or any family member, was never told I had broken my neck. We were told I had hairline fractured my C6, C7, and C8 vertebrae. When I was told that, I thought, *O.K. Sure. Whatever.* The C6, C7, and C8 vertebrae didn't mean a whole lot me.

While I was living at my parents house in Angwin, I got tired of seeing a scar on my shoulder, and not knowing where it came from. I asked my parents about it and they told me about the neck brace, and why I had been wearing it. I don't remember the brace at all, not wearing it, or even seeing it. I then asked if I had broken my neck. They said that no doctor had used those words, just the C6, C7, and C8 explanation. I don't know if I technically and/or medically had what was considered a "broken neck," but I tell people I did because it sounds cool. It makes me sound tough and real studly. It's much more impressive to tell girls, "Yeah, I had a broken neck once", than telling them, "I hairline fractured my C6, C7, and C8 vertebrae."

Anyway, I couldn't learn to walk until my neck had done some healing. I don't remember too much of this part of my healing, but there is one thing I do remember. I remember that when I did get out of bed, for whatever reason, I would have to be put in a wheelchair. Once in the wheelchair my head would have to be "tied" to a support extending upwards from the back of the wheelchair. This was because my neck muscles had "atrophied" and couldn't support my head.

I looked up "atrophy" in Webster's II Dictionary and it defined it as: "the wasting away of bodily tissues or organs." I got really tired, of hearing the word "atrophy." It seemed as if every tissue and organ had atrophied.

I would be helped out of bed and into a wheelchair. My head would then be tied to the support in back of my wheelchair. I actually liked it when my head was fastened to the support, because that allowed me to rest my neck muscles. Getting out of bed and being helped into a wheelchair, would really tire out my atrophied neck muscles, so having my head tied to the support would allow me to rest and relax. I could truly say, "I was fit to be tied."

I had to go through all this just to get out of bed and go somewhere, not that I really had anywhere to go. I remember lying in bed, day after day after day, watching TV, looking out the window and thinking, *Awww crap! This sucks!* I didn't quite realize how bad of shape I was in, I just knew I was injured and stuck in bed.

I'm a very outdoorsy kind of person. I could never really stay indoors for very long without getting all pissy, especially if the weather was good. I didn't watch much TV at all.

In the winter I would do a lot of snowboarding, when I wasn't riding a bicycle. In the summer, I would ride a bicycle, but I would also do some rock climbing whenever I got the opportunity. So it was against my very nature to stay in bed and watch TV all day. As you may imagine, it was driving me bonkers.

The rest of my stay in Acute Rehab, and therefore the hospital, is kind of a therapeutic haze. I remember what happened and a lot of the stuff I did, but the chronology of events is not really there. One reason, besides the TBI, is the fact I was indoors twenty-four hours a day, seven days a week. When you are indoors that much, the days all run together. It would have been worse had the therapy room not had a lot of windows.

I don't know when it was during all this, but I won't forget the first time I actually went outside, in what seemed like decades.

My brother-in-law is an outdoorsy kind of guy too. He wanted to take me outside for a breath of fresh air. I'm sure he must have thought I was going bonkers from being indoors so much. He was right. I think he was pretty sure it would do me good just to get outdoors and breathe some fresh air. It did.

So, I went through the whole ordeal of getting out of bed, getting into the wheelchair, and having my head tied, or fastened, to the support behind the wheelchair. I had to have some tube attached to my nose, which I assume was for breathing, but I was not hooked up to oxygen or anything else. Also, I had to wear gloves. My hands would always be freezing cold! I don't really know why, but more on that later. It was the first time I can remember that I didn't really care about all that crap, because I was going outside!

It's not like we went on some thrilling outdoor adventure, for miles and miles and days on end. I think we just went out to the parking lot and cruised around there for a while. I don't think we were outside for very long, probably only a few minutes, certainly not an hour. I didn't really care how long it was, I was outside! After I went through the reverse ordeal of getting out bed, and was comfortably back in bed, I felt as if I had run a couple marathons and then swum the English Channel. I also had a bit of a headache. I don't know what caused the headache but I have since learned one good, possible explanation.

After I got out of the hospital, I went to the eye doctor for a vision checkup. That was nothing new. I've worn glasses or contacts lenses since the fourth grade. The eye doctor noticed that my pupils didn't contract like they should when exposed to light. Therefore, I would have too much light entering my eyeball, thus causing a headache. I then realized I had been getting headaches when I went outdoors. Everytime I went outdoors, which I did as often as I could, at home, I would get a headache. Imagine if you would, someone holding your eyes open and then shining a flashlight right in them. That would cause Ray Charles to have a headache. When I first started driving, after I had been released from the hospital, I would wear my sunglasses at night because the headlights from oncoming traffic were headache producing.

When I was still in the hospital, an optometrist checked my eyes. Apparently, with injuries like mine, it's not unheard of for the optic nerve to detach. Fortunately, this was not the case with my already poor excuses for eyeballs. I have been legally blind for years. What that means is, without corrective lenses I can't tell what I'm looking at if it is not right in front of my face. However, with corrective lenses, I have better than 20/20 vision. This news of my still attached optic nerve was the first positive news I had received since I "woke up."

I promised more on the gloves, so I'll deliver on that promise. I wore gloves because my hands would be absolutely freezing cold. However, my fingers would be sweltering hot. My internal thermostat was all haywire; it was totally confused. My hands were cold, but my fingers were hot. So, I had the fingers cut off the gloves. Problem solved? Yes and no. For some reason, I scratched my legs, a lot. I would scratch skin off, hair off, little bugs off, anything and everything was scratched off. It was becoming so bad I had to wear gloves, with the fingers in tact, even though my fingers were uncomfortably hot. So, now I couldn't do any damage to myself, by myself.

CHAPTER 9

I don't remember how long I had been in Acute Rehab before I was able to get out of bed and do physical therapy i.e. learn to walk. Remember, I'm basically a large infant.

One of the first, toughest, and mentally most disturbing part of physical therapy was having to use parallel bars to walk. These are the poles that are seen on the news, in TV shows, or in movies, where a person is holding on, one in each hand, to those long, parallel to the ground, poles and struggling to put one foot in front of the other. It usually takes the person quite a while just to take a few steps. The poles were ten to fifteen feet long and it would take me quite a few minutes to go from one end to the other. After that, I was toast. I would have to go back to my room, get in bed, and rest.

I was extremely proud and a bit arrogant about my physical abilities. I had no problem making the team for any sport I tried, both in high school and junior high school. In college I wasn't on any official college teams, but I played a lot of intramural sports, and I was good at all of them. I raced mountain bikes and even raced road bicycles. I'd ridden a couple centuries on my road bicycle. A century is a 100 mile bicycle ride. So, I had no problem with anything physical.

Now, however, I couldn't even walk. It would take every calorie in my system to "walk" maybe a grand total twenty to thirty feet. I put walk in quotes because I was just leaning on the poles so I could slide one foot in front of the other. I could remember seeing stories on the news or in some TV show, about certain people or injuries, and I would see someone using those poles to walk. I would think, *Man, that must really suck. I'm glad that's not me.* Well, now it was me, and I couldn't deal with it.

I don't remember how long it would take me to do one down and back using the poles, or how many I would do at once, but I remember it would totally wear me out. I would have to go lie down in my bed, which was no easy task, and rest to get enough energy to eat. I don't think I can accurately, or adequately, describe how disturbing, or depressing, this actually was.

I also remember doing therapy, for something, using these big exercise, or therapy balls. They were soft and squishy. I would have to lean over them, face down, and also try to sit on them. When I leaned over them, face down, I would always just slide off, it was hard to breath, and a little painful. My hands and feet would just be touching the ground, and since my muscles had atrophied so much, I didn't have the strength to shift my weight around, to keep from falling off. I was too screwed up to stand on all fours, let alone walk, but you have to start somewhere and this as where I was starting. Trying to sit on them was no easier. Since my brain had been injured, my balance was below par. I would try to sit on the ball, the ball would start to roll, and I would fall off. I would realize the ball was going to roll, but I just couldn't get my body to shift the proper way to stop the rolling. That was so damn frustrating! I hated those fucking balls! I couldn't really understand why my balance was screwed up. It's pretty well known fact that their ears determine a person's sense of balance. I had no ear problems and they weren't injured in the crash. I could listen to the TV in another patient's room for crying out loud. Someone told me that since my muscles were so atrophied, they couldn't shift my weight well enough, or quickly enough, to keep up with the movement of the ball. In addition, as a result of TBI, my brain had to make knew connections. I would realize the ball was going to roll in some direction, but my muscles that would shift my weight to compensate for the roll, would not get the message, because the new connections hadn't been formed, yet. Talk about frustrating!

I was used to having very good balance. I was good on "technical" sections of mountain biking trails'; sections of trail that were not open or smooth, so you couldn't just put your head down and pedal as fast as you could. You would have to manipulate your bike around rocks, trees, and whatever else Mother Nature had put there. Sometimes it was necessary to go between large rocks or trees, through some thick mud, on some very narrow section of trail, or some combination of all this and more. In other words you would have to have good balance on your bike.

I would also do a lot of snow boarding in the winter. I liked doing half-pipes, jumps, and just going as fast as I could. All of this required balance. When I was younger I had done some snow and water skiing, both of which also require good balance.

I had one other activity that probably required more sense of balance than all of these, but you probably wouldn't think so. That activity was rock climbing. When I first started rock climbing, I used the bonehead, muscleman approach. I would get a hold of anything I could and just pull as hard as I could. At the same time, I would get my foot on anything I could and just push as hard as I could. I had been using this muscleman, jock approach for two or three years before I figured out it was much more effective to shift my weight around and "balance" myself on the rock, rather than pushing and pulling as hard as I could. For a few years I did a lot rock climbing. I climbed in Yosemite, Joshua tree, Tahoe, Mt. St. Helena, and often the Owens River Gorge. I had developed a very good sense of balance.

Now, I couldn't even sit on a big, squishy ball. I would get furious! It defined "frustrated" for me. In addition, my favorite word, "atrophy" came up again and again. It was explained to me that since my muscles used for shifting my weight had atrophied, I couldn't sufficiently shift my weight, and therefore my balance, so I would fall off the ball. Not only did this totally frustrate and piss me off, it was very depressing because my whole self-image was shot to hell. I thought of myself, prior to this "ball thing," as a very athletic and physically fit dude. If I couldn't do something that was physical, I would think that if I pushed, pulled, or whatever harder, or moved faster, I would then be able to do it. Now, this "ball thing" wasn't cooperating. It seemed the harder I tried to stay on the ball, the quicker I'd fall off. I can't describe how frustrating and maddening this was. I hated those fucking balls! I hated the word "atrophy."

CHAPTER 10

The time I spent in acute rehab is pretty much a blur now. I have memories of the therapy I did and some the of non-therapy stuff I did. I don't really remember the chronology of events, how long or how often I did them, just that I did them.

In the therapy room there was "group therapy" two or three times a week. Some of the patients would get in a circle, or group, and do some sort of therapy. The group would kick a ball around on the ground or throw and catch a large, soft ball. A small hard ball would have inflicted major damage to some of the older patients. Anyway, one day I was in group therapy and we were in a circle. A lot of the patients, including myself, were in wheelchairs, and we were supposed to kick this big ball around to one another. Sounded pretty dull to me, but I figured, *Aww. What the hell, I got nothing better to do.* It started out fine, all the patients were kicking the ball around, everything was cool. That was until the ball came to me. I sat there in my wheelchair, the ball at my feet, all the other patients in the group looking at me, I wanted to kick the ball, but my foot wouldn't move. I was thinking, *Okay, just kick the ball over to that old lady. Come on you damn foot! Just go out a little bit and hit the ball, who cares where it goes.* Well, finally my foot went out, but it missed the ball. That was pretty embarrassing. Then all the other patients gave me words of encouragement. They said things like, "Good job. You'll get it." "Keep trying." "Attaboy. That's the way." Well that just made me mad. I was an adult "jock" and I couldn't even kick a ball. To top it all off, there were a lot of older patients that seemed to have no problem kicking the ball. In my mind, they were doing something athletic better than me. I couldn't really deal with having "old" people, both men and women, doing something physical better than me. I was getting extremely upset.

So then, out of pure anger and frustration, I kicked the ball, which went up and hit some woman in the shoulder. She was fine, but the therapists put a quick halt to that session. I then told the therapists how awful everything about that made me feel. That was the last group therapy session I attended.

I also remember playing the game "Password." This was not through the hospital for some kind of therapy; it was just for a change, something different to do. I played with my oldest sister, Julianna, her husband, another sister, and my Mom. I never liked playing "Password" as a kid. I thought it was lame. I was into board games, which required less thought. Plus, I would get all upset when one of my sisters got the word and I didn't, which happened frequently.

When a family member asked me, I don't remember which one, if I wanted to play "Password," I said, "Sure. Why not." I didn't care which game it was; it was better than lying in bed watching TV. I don't remember too much of playing the game, except for one thing. I did pretty well. That totally surprised me.

I guessed the word pretty quickly on a number of occasions. I don't really know why I did well in that game. I don't like those types of games. I like games such as chess or solitaire. Maybe I did well because I was so desperate for something to do besides watch TV or do some sort of therapy.

Another thing I did in acute rehab was keep a journal. I don't know if this was some sort of therapy or some psychological nonsense, but the therapists had me keep a journal. I'm not a "journal" type of person. I remember in high school, the students of a particular class, of which I was a part, were required to keep a journal for a few weeks. I wrote down the happenings of my life for those few weeks, the night before the assignment was due. I just really didn't like writing, let alone writing every day.

However, now I thought writing a journal was the best thing going. I guess the main reason I thought it was the best thing going was that I was left alone. I wasn't doing any actual writing; I was in front of a computer "typing" it. I put typing in quotes because I wasn't really typing. I was doing the "hunt and peck" routine. This made it pretty slow going, which was fine with me, because I would be left alone while doing it. Another reason I liked it was because I got to use a computer.

I had not used a computer much previously. I had taken a computer class in high school and a General Education computer class in college, but I thought it was all for a bunch of nerds, and I was a jock. However, now it was something new, and I really like trying new things. Plus, it sure beat rolling off a big ball. I printed out everything I "wrote," and my Mom probably saved it, but I haven't looked at it. I don't really want to look at it. I have absolutely no interest in it. I "typed" it on a computer because I couldn't write very legibly yet. I was only a little kid in TBI years.

I said before that I was left alone while using the computer. I would sit in front of the computer, for what seemed like hours, hunt and peck my journal, and just listen to the scuttlebutt of the hospital. The computer was located in the large patient dining room of acute rehab, which was located in a central, well-traveled area. I heard all kinds of things. Which therapist was mad at which therapist. Which doctor was seeing who. Which therapist was having trouble with her boyfriend. All that gossipy crap. There was another patient who heard more of that gossipy crap than I did.

CHAPTER 11

There was one patient in acute rehab that got more scuttlebutt than I got. I have yet to figure out how, but he was one of those people who just seemed to know all the rumors going around. His name was Paul and he was the only person in acute rehab that was relatively close to my age. He was thirty years old and I was technically twenty-five. Paul had multiple sclerosis and diabetes; he had fallen down some stairs at home and injured himself, and so was in acute rehab.

Paul was my eyes and ears in there. He would come to my room and fill me in on everything he had seen or heard since the last time he had visited. He would usually drop by in the afternoons while I was watching one of those talk shows. We would make all kinds of comments to the TV and laugh. During all this, Paul would fill me in on the hospital gossip. He and I became friends.

Paul's mom would bring him candy every so often. He would share it with me. That was great, since the hospital food was less than scrumptious. Doing this, Paul found out I liked Gummi Bears. Every once in a while, I would get a small package of Gummi Bears from Paul. It was like Christmas! I loved getting those packages.

Whenever Paul and I would have the same therapy or exercises to do, we would do them together. One day we had to walk up some stairs; I could actually walk by now. We each had to wear a transfer/gait belt. A transfer/gait belt is a wide belt that you wear like a regular belt but it is way to long for you. A therapist holds on to the remaining belt after it is all

38

snug around your waist. The therapist holds on to the end of the transfer belt and gives you a pull if start to fall over. My therapists were all young women who were not dainty, but not buff and manly either. If I had fallen down the stairs, the only thing the transfer belt would have done, was pull the therapist down after me, thus ensuring that she fell on me and had a relatively soft landing. I could walk, but not very steadily, and the transfer belt definitely came in handy. So Paul and I were at the base of the stairs, each with a transfer belt on. We were supposed to walk the first flight, which was about seven or eight stairs. I went first. To me, the stairs looked like Mt. Everest, without the snow. I thought, *There's no way in hell I can walk up those stairs!* Fortunately the therapist holding my gait belt was very cute, so I was motivated to do well. I just it took one stair at a time, getting both feet on one stair before going to the next. It took a while. Coming down was the scary part. I could have just fallen down, that would have been the quick, easy way, but I was trying to impress the babe holding my belt. That should give you a clue to how messed up I was. I'm trying to impress a chic that has to hold on to me via a gate belt in case I fall down the stairs. I mean catch a clue!

Then it was Paul's turn. I don't think he made it up to the first landing. He would just start shaking and he just couldn't do it. The same therapist that had held on to me, was holding on to him, and she was giving him words of encouragement; as was I. Finally, he came back down and the therapy session was over.

I went back to my room, got in bed, and thought about Paul. I was getting better every day, minuscule amounts, but better. Paul was not, and probably wouldn't. It kind of freaked me out. I knew I would eventually have some sort of "normal" life, but I didn't think Paul would. I don't know if Paul thought that he would or not, but I don't think he did. I really don't think I, or anyone else, can even begin to imagine what that must be like. Anyway, on a lighter note, back to the babe therapists.

I've already mentioned Honeydew Chic, well here's another one. This babe therapist was named Kerrijoe. She was from Texas originally, so I called her "Tex." She was a brunette. On a daily basis, I had a cute blonde and a cute brunette working with me. So there I was, single, male, recently out of college, in a hospital because I was injured, surrounded by babes whose job it was to be with me in some capacity, and I was in no condition to try to impress them, which I would normally try to do. The TBI torture had begun.

I didn't give my therapists nicknames to be cute or funny. I used nicknames because I couldn't remember their real names. I got tired of seeing them and thinking, *Ooh, there's that good-looking blonde*, or *Ooh there's that cute brunette*. I would just end up saying something very intelligent like, "Hey, you" or "I forgot your name again. Now what was it?" Plus, good ol' Paul thought the nicknames were funny.

There was another cute therapist named Suzy, but I didn't work with her much. Then, to make the TBI Torture even worse, there was still another blonde therapist named Tiffany, who, in my opinion, was the best looking of all of them. I rarely got to work with her, but when I did, it was a great day. All these therapists spent a good portion of their day at work in Acute Rehab. They were all about the same age, which I think was about my age or younger. As a result of all this, they talked to each other a lot. Since I managed to be at the computer "typing" my journal often, I overheard quit a bit of what they said to each other. Since I was being TBI tortured, I often overheard them complaining about the relationships they were in. One of the therapists would complain about something her boyfriend did or didn't do. The other therapists would agree and say their boyfriends would, or would not do, the same thing.

I would just sit in front of the computer practically going insane! There I was, a young, single man, surrounded by good looking chics complaining about their boyfriends, and I couldn't even talk with them, let alone sympathize with them. I hadn't re-learned to walk very well yet, I couldn't move my wheelchair without some help, and I couldn't speak very clearly. I would get so mad I would have to go watch Rikki Lake to make myself feel better. Of course, before I could do that, I would have to wait for someone to help me get to my room. Then I would have to go through the ordeal of getting into bed. If I was lucky, the old person down the hall that couldn't hear to well, either wasn't in their room, was sleeping, or happened to be watching Rikki Lake. All this would anger me even more. Damn I was pissed! I wasn't really mad at myself; I did not hate myself, or anything else similar to that, I was just really mad at the situation I was in.

CHAPTER 12

In acute rehab there was a Dr. Green. He was a psychologist or psychiatrist; I don't know which. In case you're wondering the difference between a psychologist and a psychiatrist, I'll enlighten you. A psychologist just deals with mental issues (i.e., emotions and thoughts). A psychologist is not a medical doctor. A psychologist can't prescribe medicine for your upset stomach, fix your broken wrist, or fix a bleeding wound. A psychiatrist however, is a medical doctor. He, or she, could be your family physician and the person you talk with about your emotions and thoughts.

Dr. Green was very arrogant, had a superiority complex, and took full advantage of his last name being "Green." He always wore a green jacket or shirt and I think he drove a green car. I don't remember dealing with him much. He did give me a couple of tests and he talked with me a couple of times.

One time, he asked me if I had any guilt about what had happened to me, if I hated myself or the driver of the car, or if I was depressed. I told him I didn't feel much guilt about the accident. I realized it was, in fact, an accident and I was just at the wrong place at the wrong time. It could have happened to anyone. I didn't hate myself at all, nor did I hate the woman driving the pick up truck. I wouldn't invite her over for dinner, but I wasn't going to hunt her down and kill her either. I still hadn't quit grasped all life-changing effects of the crash would have on me, so I wasn't depressed ...yet. He asked if I felt like I should have done things differently. I thought, *Well, of course I should have done some things differently.* So I said so. But, I also knew, that me being me, would not have done anything differently. I didn't tell him that. I'm not sure how much this visit cost me, or if it was just part of the hospital bill. My parents did, however, receive a couple of bills for consultations. My parents received those consultation fees when all they had done was say, "Hi" to Dr. Green in the hallway of Acute Rehab.

Dr. Green also gave me some tests. I don't remember what the tests were testing for or how many different tests I was given. I do, however, remember one of the tests.

I was given a relatively large piece of paper with colors written on it. The names of the colors were written in a color different than the name. For example, on the paper was written the word, "blue," but the word, "blue" was written in green, or some other color. Ideally, the patient would say the word, "blue" and not the color it was written in. I felt like I did well on he test, but I never saw, or heard an actual score.

I vaguely remember getting the "ink blot test." I was shown a number of cards with a black blob of ink on them. I was then asked to describe what I saw. That is about all I remember. I don't remember any of the answers I gave or anything Dr. Green said. I was getting pretty good at tuning Dr. Green out. That alone helped alleviate my depression more than anything Dr. Green did or said.

CHAPTER 13

My stay in Acute Rehab settled into a routine. That was fine by me. It took me so much effort to do anything that I had to try things two or three times before I could actually do them. If I had kept getting new and different things to do, I'd still be in the hospital trying to do half of the stuff. That's not to say I didn't get any new things to do, but they came gradually, and I did get out of the hospital eventually.

There was one older gentleman in Acute Rehab that I really liked. His name was Ellis and I'm not real sure why he was there. I think he had a stroke. He was retired, and gray, but he was young at heart. He always seemed to be around Paul and I, the two youngest patients. Ellis had some great stories. He talked a lot.

One day I was lying in bed, with my room door open so I could hear what was going on, and see a little too. Ellis was sitting in his wheelchair in the hallway. I couldn't see him but I could hear him. "Tex" saw him sitting there and asked him what he was doing. Ellis replied, "Just sitting here watching the pretty girls." I liked Ellis even more after that.

Somewhere around this time, something happened and it was the first time I realized that I was getting better. I spent many hours in bed not doing much. As a result of this, I got many itches in every place imaginable. I could alleviate all the itches except for the itches in one spot. That spot was on my behind. I would get an itch on my rear-end, and I couldn't get my hand down there to scratch it. I don't really know why, but

I just couldn't. I would just wiggle my rear end as fast and hard as I could on my sheets and mattress, and hope for the best. Unfortunately, the best wasn't good enough. After I got tired of wiggling my butt around, I would just try to ignore it. I would channel surf really fast, then channel surf really slow, then just watch anything to try and get my mind off the itch. That had limited success. I would think of the cute nurses, or therapists. I would think of Paul or Ellis. I would think of a chemistry test in high school, anything to get my mind off the itch. The itch would not go away. I would get so frustrated and mad I wanted to scream!

Then one day, I had "The Itch." I thought, *Oh no! Here we go!* Then I just reached down and scratched it. I almost went into shock. I was so happy I almost passed out. My brother-in-law was there and so I told him. He wanted me to tell any nurse or therapist who came in. So I did. A therapist would come into my room and I would say, "I know I'm getting better. You know how I know?" The therapist would answer, "How?" I would then reply, "Because I can scratch my own ass!" The person whom I had told would laugh and congratulate me and then promptly leave. I didn't care what anybody thought, I didn't have the misery of an un-scratchable itch anymore. That was a moment of glory for me. I used to have such a moment when I placed in the top five in a mountain bike race. Now I was proud because I could scratch my own ass.

CHAPTER 14

I collided with the pick-up truck September 15, 1995. It was now Halloween. I don't like Halloween that much. I think some of the nurses dressed up a little, but that's it. We, the patients, may have gotten a cookie or piece of candy, but that's all. Since Halloween was here, that meant Thanksgiving was just around the corner. Thanksgiving has always been one of my favorite holidays. The whole family - aunts, uncles, and cousins- would get together and be a family. I would watch a lot of football, drink soda pop, drink beer when I was old enough, eat way too much, and just relax. Thanksgiving was a pretty big deal with my family. I thought about this during one of my many hours and days in bed. I thought, *Oh crap, I'll miss Thanksgiving.* Well, unbeknownst to me, I wasn't going to completely miss it. My parents, sisters, and brothers-in-law brought pizza to the hospital. They brought soda pop and even some O'douls, which is non-alchohol beer. I think they even brought some apple or pumpkin pie. We ate our Thanksgiving dinner outside in a little courtyard type place outside of Acute Rehab. I didn't miss much football either, since I had a TV right in front of me most of the day. It wasn't quite the same as the Thanksgivings I had grown up with, but it wasn't bad. At the very least, it was a break in the routine, I had some good food, and I got to go outside. By this time, my neck had recovered enough that I didn't have to have my head tied to the support on the back of my wheelchair.

Now is as good a time as any to talk about the hospital food. I don't think it really was food, it was just some substance that would keep you alive. I've never had any problem with my cholesterol level, but after eating hospital food for weeks, my cholesterol level shot way up. It's down to normal levels now, I don't recall taking any medication or being restricted to a special diet. I just quit eating hospital food. This reminds me of something.

After each meal, the patient was supposed to fill out an order form for the next meal. The form asked what we wanted for the next meal. It also asked a couple of questions about the meal we had just eaten. One question was what percentage we ate of the meal we had just been served. I'm certain the idea was for the patient to write 25%, 50%, 75%, or 100% percent. Just to give a general idea of how much was being eaten. I, however, was kind of a smart alec. I would write 98.7%, 99.12%, or 97.89%. I couldn't write 100% because there was always some crumbs or little bits of food left. The hospital staff got a kick out of the whole thing.

My favorite meal was breakfast. Even a hospital can't screw up breakfast too badly. One day, I got a pastry that didn't taste like it came from the hospital. It was really good. I wrote on my little form, "That cinnamon roll was yummy. Keep 'em coming." They did keep 'em coming. I think the hospital staff got a kick out of that too. I would get some sort of pastry every morning and would write back that it was good. I don't know where the pastries came from or if all the patients got them. I suspect that not all the patients did.

We often had dry cereal for breakfast, served in those little single-serving boxes. I love dry cereal. In college and before my crash, I had cereal almost every morning. Even now, I eat cereal for breakfast regularly. I thought it was great that I got cereal in the hospital. However, there was one problem: I could open the cereal box, but I couldn't open the little plastic inner bag that held the cereal. Every morning we had cereal, I would start my day off by getting extremely frustrated. Whichever family member was there, usually Julianna, would have to open the bag for me. I would then have to listen to whoever was there tell me that the bags were hard to open and a lot people needed help opening them. That didn't make me feel better at all. If anything, it depressed me. I think it was because I didn't like hearing that I was like other people who couldn't do something I felt was easy.

We also could have coffee. I loved coffee. At the winery where I had been working, there was coffee every morning, and I was addicted. So, not only did I get my caffeine fix every morning, I got a sweet, good-tasting pastry. I was also introduced, by a member of the hospital staff to coffee creamers: those flavored creams you add to your coffee. They come in flavors such as Irish cream, hazelnut, and French vanilla, etc. I thought they were the best thing. After I left the hospital, I continued to add the creamers to my coffee. I introduced them to my mom, and she loves them. I only drink decaf coffee now, because I became hopelessly addicted to caffeine and didn't like that.

CHAPTER 15

Somewhere along here, Ellis was able to go home. Paul and I had to do something, so we had a little get together with Ellis. We had a little table set up in the therapy room so that we could be by ourselves. Me, Paul, Ellis, and any doctor, nurse, or therapist, who happened to come by, had some cake. I don't know where the cake came from, what kind it was, or any of that.

A friend of mine was in a family that owned some vineyards. With my friend's grapes and my know-how, we had made some wine a couple of years earlier. We drank a little of this wine at our going-away get together for Ellis. The doctors had approved a little wine consumption for us, and a little was all I needed. I had, at the absolute most, two glasses of wine, and I was on the verge of being drunk. I don't know much Paul or Ellis drank, but at that point, I didn't really care. The "get-together" was about as fun as it could be for patients in the acute rehab of a hospital. It was a success and Ellis thought it was great. I said my goodbyes to Ellis and then started the long, arduous task of going to the bathroom and getting in bed. I knew the wine would make me have to pee more than usual, but Ellis was worth it.

We didn't drink much wine and I had about a case of it in my hospital room. So I gave it away. I gave some to Dr. Bodor. Some went to the nurses and therapists. I also gave a bottle to the Mexican woman who cleaned my, and the other patients, room every day. I guess she was really happy about it. She carried it around and showed everyone. She was proud of it.

I've only been told this, I didn't see any of it.

I was in another "get together." This one was not for a patient and was not planned. It just sort of happened. I don't remember who exactly was there. I was there, obviously, a couple of my sisters were there, at least one brother-in-law, and my friend Kevin. I don't remember if Kevin's future wife was there or not, I don't think she was. I met Kevin my first year at UC Davis. He was now some sort of engineer and doing some work on the Veterans Home in Yountville, which is not to far from the Queen of the Valley Hospital. He had worked that day and stopped by the hospital after he was through with work. A couple of my sisters were visiting also. My brother-in-law had to do something in Napa or was coming back from doing something in the Bay Area, and stopped by. My friend, Mike, who I have been friends with since junior high school may have been there, but I'm not certain. I was eating dinner in bed for some reason and all these people were in the room with me. I, of course, was making like the child I was, and food was going everywhere. This, of course, was a wonderful source of amusement for everyone. Once I, my sisters, my brother-in-laws, or my friends get to laughing, there's no stopping us. Jokes started flowing and humorous stories about things we've done, or seen, started rolling. I don't know how long this impromptu get-together lasted, but twice a nurse came in and told us to quiet down as other patients were trying to sleep.

When I was growing up, my parents had a subscription to *Readers Digest*. I would get the latest issue, as soon as I could, and read the anecdotes in "Laughter is the best medicine." I thought, *Laughter probably is pretty good for old people, but I doubt it's the best medicine.* Well, after that impromptu get-together, I started to think that laughter truly was the best medicine. After I laugh a lot, everything just seems better. Rotten things just don't seem as rotten. Pain just doesn't seem so painful. Life just basically seems better. This impromptu get-together certainly improved my mental health more than any psychologist or psychiatrist ever did. It was a lot cheaper too.

CHAPTER 16

I wore myself out every day, since everything took so much effort, but I would have a hard time falling asleep. I decided that music would help. I've said that I listened to heavy metal music, which is not conducive to sleep. It just so happens that I also like the music of Enya. Enya is Celtic music and very relaxing. In my hospital room I had a portable cassette player with a cassette of Enya in it. Every night, at bedtime, I would play the tape and fall asleep. The cassette player had the auto-reverse feature: that means when the cassette has completed playing one side, the player will turn in the reverse direction and play the other side. This means that the cassette will keep playing until it is stopped. Each night, when I went to bed, I would tell the nurse to stop the tape and turn off the cassette player in a couple of hours. She always did. I later learned that the nurses liked Enya so much, they would open my door and listen to the tape.

I have always liked the night, mainly because I was left alone. I also enjoyed my sleep. Now, however, I still liked being left alone, but that meant I either had to do without something, or work incredibly hard to get, or do, something. Usually whatever I wanted wasn't worth the effort, so I just did without. Another thing I didn't like about the night was that I couldn't stop thinking about "stuff." I would just think about anything and everything. I couldn't turn my brain off! I would eventually get to sleep, and sleep well.

I would wake-up, feel refreshed, and be ready for another day of therapy and gossip from Paul. At this point, I hadn't yet quit realized what was going on. The whole thing just seemed sort of like a game, or camp, or something. I didn't realize my life would never be the same. I just figured one day I'd leave the hospital and everything would be like it should. That sounds strange, by that's what I thought. I figured, *Gee, I've crashed my bike a number of times. I guess this one just happened a little worse than the rest. A few days and I'll be fine.*

I didn't really have much concept of time in the hospital. One reason, besides having a brain injury, was that I, and everyone else, was indoors for 99.9% of the time. Walls look the same at midnight as they do at noon. The main room for therapy, and the like, did have a lot of windows but it took so much concentration and effort on my part to do *anything* that I didn't notice of it was dark, light, sunny, or cloudy outside. I would just do what this "game" required and then go in my room and watch TV. The days and weeks would pass without anything changing too much and so they, and everything else, got lumped into a big amoeba of therapy. The only time indicator that really made any kind of impression on me, was that my dad cut my hair...twice.

The first time it was cut, my mom, or sister, or someone, said I was beginning to look shaggy, and needed a haircut. My dad knows how to cut hair and has cut my hair my whole life, with the exception of my college years. I thought, *O.K. It's been a while. Gee, how long have I been here? Oh well, maybe the nurses will think I look cute.* The hospital said it would be O.K. to have my dad cut my hair, in my room, so he did.

Then what seemed like a couple of days later, my mom, or sister, or someone, said I needed a haircut again. My dad gave me a haircut in my hospital room...again. I keep my hair relatively short and so get a haircut every other month or so. I remember thinking, *What is going on here?! How long have I been here? This is ridiculous! My hair needs cutting... AGAIN?!* I just didn't get it...yet.

At some point in all this, I received a package from a former college housemate. His name is Bill. I can't really describe Bill, I never could. I would just say, "Well, Bill is...just...Bill." Don't get me wrong, he is a great guy. I still stay in contact with him.

Anyway, he sent me a package. Since it was from Bill, I figured I better open it when no one was around. Problem was, I couldn't open it. My brain wouldn't tell the needed muscle to pull, or push, or whatever. Plus, my muscles had atrophied, and couldn't pull, or push, or whatever. There's my favorite word again. I think my mom opened the package. In the package were a letter and the latest issue of <u>Playboy</u> magazine. In the letter Bill wrote that he thought I could use a pick-me-up. I'm sure there was an intended pun in there somewhere.

It's uncomfortable having your mom hand you a <u>Playboy</u> magazine. I didn't know what to say, so I said, "Well, Bill is being Bill." I'm sure I looked at the magazine when everyone had gone, but I don't really remember. I do remember resting the magazine on a chair in my room. It was in plain view. All my therapist came in at some time and saw the magazine lying there. They made a few comments, but nothing too memorable. Then the magazine just sort of disappeared. I don't know when it was taken, where it was taken, or who took it. It was just gone one day. Maybe Paul or Ellis took it. I just remember that I didn't really care where it went. That, in itself, was pretty weird. It was just part of my TBI torture.

CHAPTER 17

I was just weird in acute rehab. I'm sure it was because of my brain injury, but the fact remains, there was some weird shit going on. The main weird thing was my internal thermostat went totally hay-wire. I remember being totally hot. I can't really describe how hot I was. It was as if I had temperature of 105 degrees, and was sitting in front of a campfire. It wasn't pleasant. I was sweating all the time and just plain miserable. I was seriously considering climbing into the big refrigerator in the dining room. I remember yelling at my brother-in-law to get me a "heat" doctor. I didn't know the official name of, or if there even existed, a specialist in body temperature. He said there weren't any here, meaning the Queen of the Valley Hospital. I remember yelling back, "It's a big fucking hospital! There has to be one around somewhere." I figured he had said there weren't any "heat" doctors, just to shut me up. Since I was always so hot, I had some sort pad beneath me in my bed that was supposed to regulate my temperature. Now it gets even weirder.

As I mentioned previously, my hands were freezing cold, but my fingers were hot, so I wore gloves with the fingers cut off. However, after a while, my hands and fingers were freezing cold, so I wore big, thick gloves.

Another weird thing was that I was absolutely convinced I had earplugs in my ears. I, and all the workers at the winery on the bottling line, had to wear earplugs when we worked on the bottling line. This was an O.S.H.A. (Occupational Safety and Health Administration) regulation. To wear the earplugs, the employee would just squash them up, put them in his ear, and then the earplugs would expand and plug their ears, thus blocking a lot of damaging machine noise. They were also a good excuse to ignore, something, or someone, you didn't want to deal with at the moment. I could swear I had earplugs in that I had forgotten to take out. My ears felt exactly, like they did when I had earplugs in. It didn't seem to matter to me that I could hear just fine. I knew I had earplugs in. I made such a stink over the earplugs in my ears that a doctor came and looked in my ears with a little light. He assured me that there were no earplugs in my ears. I figured he was just a quack who didn't know what the hell he was doing, because I knew there were earplugs in my ears. There weren't any earplugs, of course. I was just weird. I don't remember for how long I was convinced I had earplugs in, but it was two or three days. The earplugs eventually just sort of disappeared. I can't really describe how awful it is to be absolutely convinced you have something in your body, you can't seem to do anything about it, and no one else thinks anything is there.

As of this writing my internal thermostat is much better, but is still a little goofy. Some days I'm just hot. I feel I could stand buck naked in a blizzard, and be plenty warm. I can be sitting on the couch, watching cartoons, and just be dripping with sweat. [There's a gold mine here somewhere. I could market the "TBI Diet." For $100, I'd send you a big hammer, and some tequila. All you would have to do is, drink the tequila, hit yourself on the head with the hammer, hard enough to get a brain injury, then you could just watch TV, sweat, and the pounds would melt away. Jenny Craig would be envious of my success.]

I was hot and sweaty most of the time, but my hands and feet would get extremely cold, so cold, it would hurt. I was convinced I would get out of bed one day and my toes would have fallen off. At the very least, they would have turned black. I was just miserable twenty-four hours/day, seven days/week.

All these weird things, and some I'm sure I've forgotten about, plus therapy, therapy, and more therapy, went on for about two and a half to three months. I entered the hospital on September 15, 1995 (a day that will live in infamy) and was released on December 23, 1995.

Before I could be released, the location I was being released too, had to meet certain criteria. The location, my parent's house in this case, had to have entrances and exits that I could use. I couldn't really walk to well, so I had to be able to get in and out in a wheelchair. Fortunately, my wheelchair fit through the doorways, just barely. There was one doorway, which had only one small step, so that passed muster.

The only problem with the house was the bathroom. Since I had to pee sitting down, and I couldn't get up or walk to well, I needed something to grab onto and stand myself up. The bathroom counter was to high and not in the optimal location. My Dad said he could install a pole, from floor to ceiling, and it would be in the optimal location for me to pull myself up.

The other big problem in the bathroom was the bathtub/shower arrangement. I couldn't stand up and take a shower so I had to get a transfer bench. This is a little bench that fits in a tub, has little handles, and even a place for your soap. The patient can sit on the bench and take a shower. The patient also needs a long, flexible extension for the showerhead. This is so the patient can wash all sides of his body. It was determined that the shower in my parent's house could take a transfer bench and an extension for the showerhead.

One might think, "Well, why don't you just take baths and the hell with a shower." I wondered that to. Well, I couldn't get into or out of the tub. My balance was not very good and since my "get-up" and "get-down" muscles had atrophied, I just couldn't do it. Plus, I probably would have drowned if I had fallen over getting into or out of the tub.

My parent's house is two story, so I had to sleep, dress, and all that jazz downstairs. That was no problem because the bedroom I had until I left for college was downstairs. I would again be in the bedroom I had basically grown-up in. Weird.

The only potential problem, with the house, that could be seen was the carpet. I had a hell of a time moving around in a wheelchair on the carpet. It wasn't because my parents had thick 70s shag carpet, it was just because I didn't have the strength to push myself in the wheelchair on anything that wasn't hard and smooth. I don't really remember what was said or how the problem was solved, but it was. So my living arrangements passed hospital release muster. That was a huge relief. I had heard all sorts of horror stories about patients who had just been released from the hospital, couldn't get out of their house, and had burned in a fire. Or people whose houses hadn't been found suitable and so had to move entirely, or weren't released from the hospital until they could live safely in their current location.

The people that had looked at my living arrangements were two of my therapists. Since I was being TBI tortured, the therapists were two cute "chics." My parents had come to the acute rehab unit, picked me up and taken me home. Tex and Honeydew Chic drove separately and followed us. So there I was, young, single and being followed home by two babes. Problem was, my parents had to drive me, as I couldn't walk, couldn't talk well, and the babes were coming to see if my parents house was suitable for me to live in. It still seemed pretty cool.

It was really weird going to my parent's home after living in a hospital for fourteen weeks. When I had to leave my parents' place, my future home, and return to the hospital, I felt I was leaving a strange place and going back to where I lived. When I returned to the hospital, I felt really comfortable and relaxed. This was just mind-blowing.

The next day, while "typing" in my journal, one of my many of therapists asked me if I was scared about going home. At first I thought, *Well of course not. It's my parent's house. What a dumb question.* But then I got to thinking about it, and thought, *Holy shit! I can't do this stuff on my own!* Everything about this was really weird. Not only was I screwed up but I also had to move back in with my parents!

CHAPTER 18

C hristmas was right around the corner, or in my case, right under the bed. Wineries love holidays. Not only do they sell a lot of wine, but they have plenty of parties. The winery I was working for at the time of my incident was Flora Springs Wine Co. Flora Springs traditionally has a Christmas Dinner to which all the employees and families are invited. I was invited. Since I couldn't drive, or even walk very well, my oldest sister, Julianna, was also invited.

Mom brought me some nice clothes, and I took a shower and got all spiffed up. I had to shower at the hospital because the showers are all set up for people who can't take a regular shower. This took quite a bit of effort but I was running on adrenaline because I was getting respite from the hospital, its food, all the people I was getting tired of looking at, and I was going someplace I really wanted to go.

Julianna came and picked me up, we put my wheelchair in her car, and then we left. Not being in the hospital it seemed surreal. There were Christmas lights and decorations in a lot of people's yards. There aren't many Christmas decorations in the hospital. As we got closer to the winery, I wasn't really scared, but I almost started crying.

My sister said we didn't have to go, we could turn around and go back. I said, "No. Let's go." I didn't want to have put in so much effort and not go, and I didn't really want to have to tell everyone why I was back so soon. So I did the manly thing and sucked it up. We continued on.

Flora Springs is a small winery. I worked in the cellar with just one other guy, Paul, but everyone called him Pauli. He was the first person I saw upon arriving at the winery. We said "Hello" and all that stuff and then he grabbed my wheelchair out of my sister's car, and started unfolding it. I was used to having Pauli help me move oak barrels, which are darn heavy. We would also move hoses, pumps, and bottling equipment. A lot of the work in a winery cellar is physical and requires strength. Now, the guy whom I had been doing this type of work with for about a year, was getting a wheelchair ready for me to sit in. It was strange seeing Pauli fighting with a wheelchair, but even stranger was the fact that the wheelchair was for me. That's when it started to hit me.

I was wheeled into the tasting room, which is where the dinner was held. There were six tables with five or six people at each one. The meal was really good; of course, having eaten hospital food for a few weeks would have made sweat-covered lima beans taste good. I don't remember much about the dinner, except I had to tell everyone I was still alive and getting better. I tried not to say much because it was difficult for me to speak understandably. Also, I was absolutely dreading having to use the bathroom. I didn't want to embarrass myself by needing help to get into or out of the bathroom, or even worse, to need help getting on and off the toilet. I kept my liquid intake as minimal as I could for dinner, but…I had to pee.

I actually stood up and walked into the bathroom. At least I'm pretty sure I did, because, although the bathrooms are equipped for the handicapped, the doorway is narrow and I don't think I could have gotten in there with my wheelchair without help. I didn't want too ask for help from anyone; it was pride, or fear, or wanting to be "normal," or not wanting anyone to know I had to sit down to pee. Whatever it was, I was determined to walk into the bathroom. So I did. It was a pretty short walk but still a walk. I relieved myself, and then rejoined the party. Talk about a weight coming off your shoulders! I think I even had a glass of wine. A small glass, but still a glass.

In college, I heard the phrase, "a cheap date." I knew what it referred to but it always referred to a woman. If you don't know what it means, I'll explain it...nicely. Guys would refer to a "chic" as a cheap date if you could get her drunk on just a couple of drinks, and then, of course, she would be very agreeable with you. Well, I was a cheap date now: one small glass of wine and I would have agreed to just about anything. I wasn't drunk, I was just mellow and agreeable, it felt very nice.

When it was time to leave, I got back into my sister's car. Pauli helped Julianna put my wheelchair in the car and then we left. The winery is about twenty-five to thirty minutes away from the hospital. During the drive back to the hospital, everything hit me. I realized that my life was pretty well fucked-up! We arrived back at the hospital around 10:00 P.M. That is pretty early for a winery party to be over, and even earlier for a young, single guy to be calling it quits for the night. However, I was not a young, single guy. I was a five to seven TBI-year-old little squirt. The Acute Rehab unit, my home, was quiet, empty, and lifeless when we arrived. I went through the whole ordeal of getting out of the car, into my wheelchair, into my room, out of the wheelchair, out of my clothes, into my pajamas, and then into bed.

It kept hitting me that my life was still pretty well screwed up. I knew that working in a winery was gone. I missed those people. I can honestly, say that I loved my job. I've heard that a lot of people become depressed on Sunday nights because they have to go to work the next day. Not I. I looked forward to Sunday nights, because that meant I was going to work the next day, doing what I loved to do, and being with people I enjoyed being with. I also looked forward to Friday's because that meant I could spend the next two days riding my bike. I was truly happy with my life, with one exception: I was tired of being single, so I was making an effort to do stuff with women I was attracted to. Hence, I had been bicycle riding with a girl. Now that was all gone.

I just lay in bed and cried, for at least a day, maybe two. I don't remember too much, except for two things. One: I didn't have to get out of bed and do any therapy, or anything else for that matter. Two: some therapist, or nurse, just stood by my bed and rubbed my neck for what seemed like hours. I don't really know why she did it, or anything like that. I just know it felt good and I'm glad she did it.

I found out later that the hospital staff was relieved that I had finally broken down. I guess it is expected and is a necessary step for the healing process. The acute rehab staff was beginning to wonder about me. Well they didn't wonder anymore. I lost it.

I don't know how or when I got myself together, but I did. I think it was the fact that I knew I was leaving the hospital soon and going home. I know what didn't have absolutely anything to do with me getting it together: the psychologist, Dr. Green, whose job it was to help people in my situation. On second thought, maybe he did, indirectly, have something to do with it. I pulled it together as best I could so that I wouldn't have to deal with him. He was that annoying.

CHAPTER 19

I had recovered, physically, enough to be released from the hospital. But before the "Big Day" the therapists and the doctor in charge, Dr. Marco Bodor, had a little going away party for me. I don't remember what we ate or drank, but I was given a couple of gifts and I do remember those.

From the therapists, I got a T-shirt that the therapists had all signed, and Honeydew Chic had even drawn a bunch of coffee stains on it. They also gave me a book of bathroom jokes to read because they knew it took me quite some time to "relieve" myself. This gift-giving didn't just go one way. My brother-in-law, who is a photographer, gave Dr. Bodor a large, framed, photo he had taken of Yosemite Valley covered with a thin layer of fog, at dusk. Dr. Bodor really liked it. I certainly didn't want to end up in the hospital, but since I did, I'm glad the people who were there, were there. That wouldn't be the last I saw of Dr. Bodor.

The shindig was only a couple of days before I was released from the hospital. Those couple of days are a blur to me. I'm sure there was physical therapy. Dr. Green probably saw me. There are, however, two questions I was asked by a couple of therapists that I certainly remember.

The first question was, "Are you afraid to be going home?" I thought, *Are you serious? Afraid to be going home? Of course not! Get real.* But as the day approached, I would have been shaking in my boots, had I been able to walk well enough to need boots. I started thinking, *What if can't get in and out of the bathroom? What if I fall off the toilet? What if I can't get in or out of bed? Am I going to be stuck inside? Am I going to get any better? How is my speech going to get better? Is my speech going to get better? How am I going to deal with my parents? What will my friends think? Will I have any friends? Will I have to do therapy at home? What are showers going to be like?* That's just the tip of the iceberg as far as questions I had.

The second question, at first, seemed even more ridiculous. That question was, "Are you going to miss this place?" I thought, *Aww. Come on! You can't be serious! Miss all this shit?! Of course not! I can't wait to leave! I never want to see it again.* As they day approached, however, I thought, *Ya know, at home I won't have all these people at my beck and call.* In Acute Rehab if I wanted something to drink or snack on, or if I was uncomfortable in any way, I pressed my little "nurse call button" and eventually a nurse would come. There was always at least one cute nurse around. I was going to miss seeing "Honeydew chic" and "Tex." I was going to miss seeing Tiffany and Suzy. *Was I going to see any women aside from my Mom?* That thought alone freaked-me-out pretty well. No offense Mom. I could honestly say I was going to miss the place.

I was going into a very familiar house with very familiar people, except now, it seemed, as though it was a great unknown. That alone, was just…weird. I really didn't know if I could, in fact, get by in a house that wasn't all set up for someone with handicaps. I had handicaps, still do. It was freaking me out!

The guy who had grown up in the house, spent most of his life there, was very familiar with the people whom he'd be living with, was no longer alive. The "child" who looked just like him, was *not* just like him. Close, but not the same. He was just a little bit skewed. Plus, he was only a few years old, TBI years mind you, but still a child in many ways.

So the day came. It was December 23, 1995. I was admitted to the hospital on September 15, 1995. I don't remember what time I left but I think was early afternoon. The part of that day before I left is pretty much a blur. I'm sure I ate something. I said "Bye" to all the hospital staff that I wanted to. I was put in my wheelchair and pushed out to my parent's car. As we were driving away, I waved goodbye to Tex, Honeydew Chic, Tiffany, and a couple of other therapists.

CHAPTER 20

All the way home, I couldn't believe I was actually out of the hospital and going home. No more hospital food. No more hearing the "bing" of the little bell that rang when a patient pushed the little button to call the nurse.

That reminds me. In Acute Rehab when a patient wants, or needs, something they press a little button. When they do so, a light goes on, in the hallway, above the door of the patient who "rang." Accompanying the light is a "bing" noise, I assume to alert the nursing staff they are needed. That little "bing" nearly drove me fucking nuts! All night I'd hear "bing", "bing", "bing", "bing", "bing." I swear that "bing" sound went on through the entire night. I would get furious! Of course, if I wanted or needed something I would have to press my own button and make my own "bing" noise. I couldn't just get out of bed and get it, so I just did without. That just added to my already infinite frustration, if that is possible.

So anyway, no more "bing." It was blowing my mind how nice that was going to be. I really couldn't quite believe it. It was like the Twilight Zone, or something. We drove into the yard of my new home and it was almost surreal. I just couldn't quite fathom not being in the hospital *and* living with my parents. I can't adequately describe what I was thinking. It was just...weird.

We parked the car, and got out. All except for me, of course, I needed some help. I was helped out of the car, into my wheelchair, and up to the door with only one stair. By now I was getting headache from all the "new" surroundings. Just having to be in a wheelchair to get around in the same surroundings I had spent a majority of my life in, was just causing my brain to scream for help. Problem was, no one could hear it except for me, and my body couldn't respond. I think that's when the depression started.

Anyway, I got up the one stair, with some help, and got in the house. Even that was a bit of a "trip" because in all the years I had lived with my parents, I had used that particular entrance maybe ten times per year, and now I had to use it, because that was the only one I *could* use. I got in the house and it was…just…really…strange. I don't know why, it just was. The only thing I can think of is that I had been "born" three and half months earlier but my body and parts of my brain were twenty-five years old. The only thing the "new" me knew was the hospital. The hospital was literally the only life the "new" me had ever known, but the "old" me had spent the majority of his life in this house.

So, I got myself in the wheelchair and into my new home. The first problem was pretty quickly realized. I couldn't move my wheelchair around on the carpet without some help. I would put every ounce of strength I could muster into my arms, push the wheels, and maybe, at best, move a couple of feet. So, I would need some help to go around the house. I don't really remember much of this day, except that I was not in the hospital.

I remember one part of the day like it just happened. That part is, my first bedtime. I don't know why, exactly, but it is etched my memory, permanently: I couldn't brush my teeth. My sister had to brush my teeth for me.

My sister that is closest to me in age, except for the twin, was going through a divorce and so was living at home with me. She would brush my teeth. I'm not sure why I couldn't brush my own teeth, except maybe I lacked the coordination for it. I remember it was so disturbing to need to my sister to brush my teeth that I would just laugh. I couldn't stop. Everyone thought it was cute and would start laughing also, but that just made it worse. It was so embarrassing I couldn't really deal with it. It doesn't get much better.

I was all ready for my first night at home; I just needed to get in bed. So I was helped into bed, which was okay. However, when I actually lay down, I whacked my head on the back of the bed frame. So from then on, whenever I laid down for sleep, my mom would put her hand on the back of my head. It was reminiscent of the way you see policemen put their hand on the head of someone in handcuffs that is being put in a police car. I liked going to bed, because that meant another day was gone, but I hated going through the bedtime ordeal. I hated having my Mom put her hand on the back of my head when I laid down to go to sleep. I was only a small child in TBI years, so my Mom's hand was needed to prevent me from whacking my head on the bed frame. I just didn't get it. My brain didn't have the organization or capacity yet to realize that if I were sitting to close to the back of the bed, I would hit my head when I lay down. So, part of me, the TBI child, was glad my Mom's hand was there, but part of me, the grown man part of me, was insulted and infuriated by it.

As you can well imagine, bedtime was not my favorite time of day. The only good thing about bedtime was that the day was over, and I was one day closer to death. I would just hope, I mean really hope, that I would never wake up. I always would, of course. As I said before, I listened to hard rock "music." There is a quote from a heavy metal song by the band Pantera that is just perfect. It is: "Yesterday don't mean shit because tomorrow's day you have to face." This song wasn't even written at this point in my life, but when I heard it, a couple of years later, it just hit the nail on the head.

Whenever I complained about something people would just say, "You've had a terrible accident, you're doing very well." I would think, *You know, I don't really care why I'm not happy with any aspect of my life. The fact is, my life is just miserable.* I was totally depressed. I didn't care if I lived or died. As I'm writing this, I still don't care.

You may be thinking, "Why do you think that way? Who knows what will happen? If you're dead, nothing good will happen. That is for sure." Well, I didn't think anything was going to happen anyway. You'll see later some really awful things that did happen. Back to bedtime.

After I completed the ordeal, both mentally and physically, of getting into bed, I would sleep. I would wake up in the morning feeling refreshed and ready to tackle another day of therapy and complete depression.

At first, a couple of therapists came to my parent's house to work with me. They made house calls. I had a speech therapist come to the house, I also had an occupational therapist or a physical therapist, maybe both, I don't really remember. I do remember one of the therapists, mainly because she just pissed me off so much. She was an occupational or physical therapist, I'm not sure which. She had me doing stuff I had never done much of before my accident, so I wasn't very good at it, but she insisted I do it. I would get extremely frustrated. She had me folding clothes, doing dishes, vacuuming, and she also had me making sandwiches. I hated doing therapy and basically fought it. I ended up in a worse mood than I was in when she came. It just gets worse.

One of my "exercises" was to stand a quarter on its side, or edge, on a table with a tablecloth. It is possible to stand a quarter on its edge on a hard, smooth surface. I've done it...once. I don't think it's possible on a tablecloth, and I told my therapist. She didn't like that. There are too many variables, not the least of which is the condition of the edge of the quarter. I would sit there with my therapist, for what seemed like hours, trying to stand a quarter on its edge on our kitchen table, which had a tablecloth. I couldn't do it and so would just get so pissed-off and frustrated that I couldn't think straight. It's not good when you are in a condition that requires a therapist to come to your house. It's even worse when you end up getting upset and frustrated doing the therapy. It would take me the rest of the day to calm down. Then I would have to go through the whole "getting ready for bed" ordeal, which would just frustrate me more. As the reader might guess, I was a very frustrated person...still am.

There is one other thing I had to do at bedtime, but I'm not sure when I started doing it, so I'll just tell you now. I had to wear braces on my ankles. My feet were not at 90-degree angles to my legs. They were just kind of in a straight line. This was probably because my ankle muscles had atrophied. The braces I wore held my feet at basically right angles to my shins. They did not hurt, they were just a bit uncomfortable. Now that I think about it, I had to wear the ankle braces all the time, not just to bed. They weren't painful to wear, just a little uncomfortable and cumbersome.

So, I'm finally ready to sleep. I'm in bed, all the embarrassing aspects for the night are over. It's just me lying in bed with my thoughts. That was not good. I would think how awful my life was. How I was living with my parents, I had no job, much less a career, I didn't have a girlfriend, or even a potential girlfriend, I basically had nothing. I would also think about what type of therapy I had the next day, and if done all the exercises I was supposed to have done.

There is one other thought I would have every night. I would hope for a tree to fall through the house and kill me. I didn't want to live. I had no future, and the present was pretty bleak! I would also think of other ways I could "accidentally" be killed. If I thought of one that was semi-probable, I would think of ways to increase the chances of it happening. I would then think of what the next day would bring, and gee...it was more therapy. If I sound depressed, that's because I was.

CHAPTER 21

I would, and did, eventually fall asleep on my first night out of the hospital. I don't remember much except that it was just really strange living at home again. It was the first night of my entire life out of the hospital. I was born on September 15, 1995 and now it was December 23, 1995. I don't really know how old I was in TBI years, but it wasn't very old. I was just a little kid.

The next day, Christmas Eve, included absolutely no therapy, which was fine with me. I was in the hospital for three and a half months and it seemed all I had done was therapy. I was on vacation. Besides my therapy would begin soon after Christmas.

The day was pretty much a whirlwind. I just couldn't believe I was living at home. First of all, I had a breakfast that was not hospital food. I do not remember what I had, except for the fact that it was actual food. I felt my cholesterol level go down. Then I just remember sitting in my chair in different places, inside the house, and thinking, *Holy cow! I'm living here! Boy, I must really be fucked-up!* I also remember I needed to lie down and take a nap in the early afternoon, as I was just worn out, both mentally and physically. I also had to rest because I had a big night ahead of me.

It was Christmas Eve and therefore, I had a lot of presents to deliver. No, just kidding. Well, it was Christmas Eve and I was going to a big family dinner at my aunt's house. Christmas Eve dinner has been a tradition in my family for many, many moons and I wasn't about to break any traditions. So I rested.

Getting ready to go was a major undertaking. I had to get clean. So I got naked and was helped onto my transfer bench. I couldn't yet wash myself, so someone had to wash and rinse me. I was then helped off the transfer bench and dried off. My brother-in-law was responsible for all my hygiene on this particular day. I don't remember how long in terms of minutes, or hours, this cleaning ordeal took, but it seemed like hours.

So here I was, a previously very athletic, cocky, healthy, totally independent guy, being washed by his brother-in-law with whom he had raced mountain bikes and climbed many 'o rock with. Needless to say, I was not in the giving or receiving mood after this. Well, maybe giving someone, or something, a good swift kick, but that was about it.

I was finally ready to go, I was helped out to, and into, my parents car and off we went. My aunt and uncle live in Napa. The same town of the hospital I'd been in for three and a half months. I felt like I was going home. We arrived at my aunt's house and it was Twilight Zone-ish. Everything just seemed strange. Everyone and everything was very familiar yet everything seemed brand new. I found a nice, comfy chair and just sat there. I said "Hi" to anyone who passed by, but I didn't talk much. Mainly because it was extremely difficult to speak understandably, but also because I didn't like to hear myself. I didn't like to hear myself because it was really depressing. Why was it depressing? Well, I'll tell you.

No matter how hard I tried and how much I concentrated on it, my speech would come out less than…intelligent sounding. I would try to talk to someone and all they would say was, "What? Huh? Say that again." I felt like someone who was totally retarded. It was not good. I never talked much at family gatherings before, but that was by choice. If I chose to say something, I would, and could say it. Now, however, I could not really do that. I felt like was forced to be quiet.

I just sat in a comfy chair and had people get me egg nog. We didn't have a formal, sit-down dinner, we just ate whores ovaries (hor d'ouveres). I didn't do much socializing, or anything else for that matter. I just sat in my chair and watched and listened. It was pretty lame but that is about all I could do. The night couldn't end soon enough. Fortunately, it did end. Gee, then it was time to go through the ordeal of getting in the car. I went through that ordeal and then the ordeal of getting out of the car, ready for bed, and then into bed.

We had hung our stockings above the fireplace before we had gone to my aunt's house. Well, everyone but me. I physically couldn't do it. Someone did it for me. All this pretty much sucked, but I didn't really care, because I knew I was getting an Apple Macintosh for Christmas.

My Grandmother knew I had enjoyed "typing" my journal on a computer in acute rehab. I think she also knew I could play games and do other things on a computer. Since I was going to be stuck at home, she figured I could probably use a computer. So she got me a Macintosh. I couldn't wait until Christmas morning!

Well, it became Christmas shortly thereafter. I got out of bed, no simple task, and into my wheelchair and helped to where the stockings were. I was still alive and not too pleased. Someone had to get my stocking for me, which was like starting the day with a good, swift kick in the crotch, but I didn't really care, because was getting a computer.

I suffered through emptying the stockings, having breakfast, getting dressed, and all that jazz. Then we opened our presents. I didn't actually "open" my computer, it was already all set up for me by my brother-in-law. Now, however, it was "officially" mine. I don't really remember when I first used it or what I first did, probably played some game. I just remember it was cool and I was happy. That was the first time I was happy with anything since my accident. Now, it was time for all the relatives to start appearing and the traditional Christmas meal to be eaten.

Eventually, in what seemed like days, it was time to eat. I could eat regular food, but not very cleanly. I had to use my left hand, or at least help my right hand with my left, so I was pretty good at making little messes with my food. Not that this really bothered me, or anything, it was just kind of annoying. As a result of all this, I just couldn't relax and enjoy myself, or the food.

One thing I do remember, however, is that the parents of the girl I had gone riding with prior to my collision, stopped by and brought a gift; not just for me, it was some snack type thing, I don't remember what it was. I probably had no clue what it was anyway. I just thought it was strange they had stopped by and brought something. It was nice, but strange.

I also remember wanting everyone to leave me alone so I could fool around with my computer. Being left alone is a pretty rare treat when you can't even brush your own teeth.

CHAPTER 22

After Christmas, my life (if you could call it that) was shoved into a pretty dull and boring, but therapeutic, routine. I spent a lot of time doing therapy, fooling around on my computer, reading, and watching TV. After I left the hospital, I had absolutely no desire to watch Ricki Lake or any of those types of shows. I just couldn't stomach them, I can't to this day.

I had therapists come to my parents house for my therapy. I don't remember too much of it except for the one therapist, Claire, who was the previously mentioned therapist that wanted me to stand a quarter on its edge on a tablecloth. This therapy only lasted for a few months. After this therapy "stage" was completed, I was to go to the St. Helena Hospital and Health Center for more therapy.

One of my therapists, during this time, suggested that once my therapy at the St. Helena Hospital and Health Center started, I should take a nap, or at least rest before going to my therapy session, as it would be very taxing for me. Well, my first day for therapy at the hospital arrived. So I took a nap and then went to therapy. My Mom had to drive me, as I couldn't drive yet. Even with all the home therapy I had received, I still couldn't walk to well and I couldn't put my contact lenses in. Therefore, I had to use my wheelchair and wear my glasses. In TBI years, I was in my early teens. As a result, I was extremely self-conscious. Like most teenagers, I was very concerned about how I looked and came across to people. I didn't want people to think I was "weird." I didn't like to be in public, in any capacity because all I could think of was how messed-up people thought I must be. I was in a wheelchair and very self-conscious of that. I had to wear my glasses and was self-conscious of that. My speech was less than fluent. I sounded like I was very dumb, drunk, and retarded. I was very self-conscious of that. I won't even mention how I thought women must perceive me. So, I didn't like to have to go to a hospital and get therapy, mainly because people would see me.

I had one small, consoling thought about going to the hospital. That was: *At least there probably won't be any good-looking chics there. It'll just be middle-aged married nurses and/or some dorky dudes. At least then I won't be embarrassed* Well, guess what? The most incredible woman I've ever seen was a physical therapy assistant at the hospital. Her name was Julie and I was in love. Problem was, I was totally messed-up! I was in the absolute worst condition I was ever in, plus I was basically a teenager and I had no clue what to do. I had lost all of my social skills, knowledge… everything. I had basically been re-born a few months earlier and spent my whole "life" alone. I spent three and a half months in the hospital, basically alone. I was now living with my parents, so I was alone for all intents and purposes. I hadn't had any type of interaction with a female, except for therapy, in my whole "life." Now, I was to have therapy around Julie. My head almost exploded! TBI torture was reaching a whole new level.

I had one saving grace...I thought. Julie was wearing a wedding ring, so I figured she was married, so, my tough luck. When you are a single male, recently out of college, living on your own, have a good job, and you're tired of drinking beer and trying to pick-up chics, you start to notice things like which girls are wearing wedding rings. With me, the girls who were wearing wedding rings were off limits. With Julie I thought, *Oh well. I wish I had met her a couple years ago.*

Now, Julie was just an assistant therapist, so I didn't work with her very much, but she was around a lot. I actually looked forward to going to my therapy appointment, so I could see

Julie. I know I sound pretty pathetic and desperate, but hell, I was both. I said before that I had to wear my glasses because I couldn't put my contacts in. Putting a piece of plastic on your eyeballs requires pretty fine and delicate movements. All of which I didn't have because of my brain injury. However, I was determined to get them in because I wanted Julie to see me without my glasses. You must remember, in my TBI life I was just a young teenager, but in reality, I was a college graduate, living with his parents, who had been in the hospital for three and a half months. So I was pretty desperate.

So I would get everything I needed to put my contacts in, sit down, and try to put them in. Normally, I would put them in standing-up. I would just lean forward, over the bathroom counter, look in the mirror and put them in. I would put them in using my right hand, as I was right handed. Now, however, since my right deltoid muscle, and therefore my shoulder, were pretty useless, I had to put them in sitting down with a little travel mirror so could lean on a table and support my right elbow. I couldn't get them in. I would get so frustrated and furious! I would try to put them in for an hour or so just cussing really loud and getting more and more frustrated the whole time. I kept thinking that all I wanted was to see Julie, and therefore her see me, with my contacts in.

I would try to put them in for an hour or so. I couldn't try much longer than that because my voice would give out from screaming obscenities, and I would get so frustrated, that I could hardly function, let alone think straight.

Putting Julie aside, for now, I actually did a lot therapy at the hospital. I don't remember a whole lot of it, but I do remember one thing. I don't remember if this was occupational therapy or physical therapy. I just remember I hated it. I had to put these round pegs into little holes. At least they weren't square pegs.

I also remember doing a therapeutic activity that was kind of fun. There was one of those small, round, trampolines that I would tilt up so that the trampoline was at about fifteen to twenty degrees. I then would take a weighted ball and throw it at the trampoline. The trampoline would then "throw" the ball back, in the air, and I would try to catch it. I would throw the weighted ball with my right hand in order to work my right shoulder, thereby working my right deltoid muscle. I got so I could throw the ball well enough to hit the trampoline, but I couldn't catch the returning ball to well. I could catch it if the ball came right back to me, but it rarely did. I couldn't move very fast, for whatever reason, and I spent a lot of time watching it go right by me. There were balls of varying weights, from very light to a pound or so. I started out with one of the lighter balls and worked my way up to the heavier balls. This was one exercise that I could understand how it would help me and it was kind of fun, so I actually enjoyed it, even though I spent most of the time watching the ball go past me.

I'm sure there is a medical explanation for my lack speedy movement, but all I know is I would just get really frustrated. I couldn't run. As of this writing, I still can't run. I don't know if it's because of brain damage, atrophy, or simply just incredible stiffness. The fact remains, I just can't run. If someone put a gun to my head and told me run, or even jog, or else they going to pull the trigger, I'd say, "Well, you might as well pull it now. It'll save us both some time, because I just can't run." I don't know why I can't run. It's a pretty natural human ability. I would just get so furious that I couldn't see, or think, straight!

I remember doing something else. I would lie on my back, on a table, and try to raise my right hand to the ceiling. I couldn't do it because of my right deltoid muscle, or lack thereof. My therapist would raise my hand for me but I couldn't keep it there, unless, I was holding on to some object, i.e. a stick, broomhandle, or something similar. My therapists didn't know why, they just thought I was weird. We did find that if my right arm was put in an air cast, and the cast was inflated, I was able to hold my hand up towards the ceiling without having to hold on to any object. Again, I was thought to be strange. Which was fine with me. I didn't really mind lying on the table trying to do this because Julie was usually nearby and I thought she was a total babe! Of course I was in no shape to impress her, but I was usually so mad, and/or frustrated, at something that I wasn't thinking straight, so I thought I could impress her.

I don't remember how long I had therapy in the therapy room, it seemed like years, but eventually the pool was ready to be used. I would now have therapy in the pool sometimes. I think it was once a week, but don't quote me on that. At first, I had to be pushed in my wheelchair out to the covered pool. I couldn't walk to well yet. Well, I could walk, but not very far. My body would just give out. Plus, my balance was so..."unbalanced" that I couldn't go up, or down, a stair, much less stairs. So I would get in my swim trunks, which was harder than it sounds, get in my wheelchair, and be helped down to the pool. My therapist, Christy, helped me down.

Therapy in the pool was pretty cool, pun intended. I couldn't fall over; well I could, but I wouldn't hit the ground. At first, I would just walk around the pool, inside of course. I actually felt like I accomplished something. When you walk in water, every movement you make is met with resistance. Therefore, a lot of your muscles are worked. The word "atrophy" should be in here somewhere.

Another thing I did was jump off the steps going into the pool. I started at the lowest step, so I was more than half-way in the water before I jumped. I worked my way up the stairs and eventually "jumped" off the side of the pool. I put "jumped" in quotes because I wasn't really jumping. I was just sort falling over as best I could into the water. This was just as frustrating as trying to raise my right hand. I thought jumping was a pretty simple thing. You just bend your knees, push upwards, and lean forward. Sounds simple. Well, that's what I thought. I could bend my knees fine. However, that's about as far as my brain had gotten. I would start to push upwards and my brain would just say, "O.K. that's it. I quit!" I would begin to push upwards, I would lean forward and then...nothing. I would just fall in the water. Even pushing upwards was a little sketchy. I didn't seem to push upwards with both legs. I only had the brain power to activate one leg at a time. I could push myself upwards with one leg, either one, but not the other. I guess my brain only had the capacity to control one leg at a time. Then throw into the mix that I had to shift my weight forward while operating a leg, and I really had no idea what was going to happen. "Jumping" from the lower steps was no problem, in terms of fear. However, when I was going off the higher steps, and eventually the side of the pool, fear definitely entered into the equation. Fear is an incredibly powerful motivator, for me anyway.

When I first started therapy in the pool, I was still wearing my glasses, as I could not yet put my contact lenses in. When I was "jumping" off the steps or side of the pool, I had to take my glasses off. I'm legally blind. So, without my glasses, the pool was just a blue blob and everything around me was totally fuzzy and blurry. I'm sure this somehow added to my fear. But I did not really care because this was supposed to help me get better and I figured, *Oh what the hell, I'm at a hospital. If I get hurt, I won't have to go very far.*

I did do other therapeutic activities in the pool. I took my glasses off for this stuff to. I had to hold a ball that would float, underwater, and try to balance myself well enough so that I could sit on it. I could not do it and the ball would go shooting to the surface and float away. I, of course, had to retrieve it and try it again.

I also had to hold a kickboard and kick around the pool. It was a lot harder than it sounds. It was hard to kick with both legs one after the other, as when you're swimming. I could kick with one leg, either one, by itself with no problem. However, when I had to use both legs, one after the other, I just could not do it. I would think, *O.K., kick your right leg, then your left, then right, then left...,* but my legs just would not do it separately. If I got one leg to kick, I couldn't get the other one to go without stopping the first one. I would get so angry! I would also fall off the kickboard. I did my kicking exercise while holding on to the kickboard under my chin. Problem was, I could not keep the kickboard flat. I would turn sideways and go underwater. I was learning how to swim again except I knew that I already knew how to swim. I can't begin how to describe how frustrating it is to know that you know to do something, yet you can't do it. I would think, *O.K., you have to do X, Y, and Z in order to swim.* As a result of my TBI, my body just wouldn't do what I was telling it to. It would respond, so I knew it was getting a message, but it was misinterpreting the message. The only thing that kept me from getting totally fed-up with it and quitting was I knew it would eventually help me get better, and that was all I wanted.

I'll have to jump out of time here and say something. Throughout my recovery, I have seen a number of doctors, therapists, psychologists, etc. More than once, I have heard from a "professional," that I must not want to get better. I heard this after a doctor, or therapist, or whomever failed at solving whatever problem, or pain, I was seeing the person for. When my problem failed to be solved by the suggested exercise, medicine, or device, the individual who had made the suggestion would just tell me that I must not really want to get better. I really couldn't comprehend the arrogance this line of thinking would come from. That's saying something, because I know arrogance, as I was a very arrogant individual. I know a lot of very arrogant individuals, but these "professionals" took the cake. I would get furious! I was bordering on homicidal! I would think, *You have no fucking clue what I want! The **ONLY** thing I want is to get better! So don't sit there and make yourself feel better by explaining that your failure to help me is my fault.*

Enough of that, so back to therapy. There is one more therapeutic activity that I did in the pool that frustrated the hell out of me. I would use these long, cylindrical, flotation, torture devices. Well, they weren't really torture devices, but they sure could have been for me. I would take one torture device, bend it so that I had each end under a different arm, to form a "U" shape, put it under water, and try to sit on it. I couldn't do it. I had a hell of a time trying to put it under water while keeping it in a "U" shape. I would get it in the right shape after a lot of silent cussing. However, every time I tried to sit on it, I would fall over and the torture device would float away. Thus, I would have to start all over again. I would get so upset and frustrated, I thought the pool water would start to boil.

The therapist who accompanied me into the pool was named Christy, and I think she could tell how frustrated I would get and she mercifully would stop having me use the torture devices. There was a different pool activity that I enjoyed. I was not able to do this activity until the latter part of my therapy. I had re-learned to swim at that point. Christy would throw a few small, colored rings into the pool. The rings would sink to the bottom of the pool. I would walk in the pool until I found a ring, then I would swim down and get it. I actually enjoyed this. It was fun.

There was one other therapist working there. His name is Ron. I've known Ron since I was in kindergarten. He and my Dad are friends. They go hunting and fishing together. I have gone with them. Ron did some work with me in the pool. It was fine, but really strange. It could have been really depressing except that I've always gotten a kick out Ron.

CHAPTER 23

When I was not doing some sort of therapy, I was at home trying to keep sane. I was an adult living at home. Technically, I was 25 years old, but in reality, or TBI years, I was just a teenager. As is common with a lot of teens, my parents annoyed me. Like most teens, I couldn't drive yet, had no income, and was very dependent on my parents. I could not really cope with it, so I just engulfed myself in my computer. I could sit for hours in front of my computer and just be fooling around i.e. I wouldn't really do anything productive. My parents are pretty "old school." They had no interest in computers and so would leave me alone when I was using my computer. I played a lot of games, but I did learn something potentially valuable. I learned HTML, Hyper Text Markup Language, which is the language the World Wide Web speaks

While surfing the web one day, I came across a program that I could download and create my own web page. So I did. The best part of doing this was that it took a lot of time and my parents stayed out of my hair. Therefore, my sanity was kept pretty much intact. It also gave something for my mind to do, besides think about how screwed-up my life was. So, without further adieu, here it is. You knew it was coming: http://members.aol.com/ggooseiiii/headinjury.html. It's the website I made about my bike crash. It seems that there is nothing that does not have web address associated with it.

I also got into chat rooms often. I "met" some girls, at least I think they were girls. My entire social life was doctors, therapists, or parents. That's not good at any age, but especially not as a teenager. I was never a very social person. I liked to play golf, ride bicycles, work in a wine cellar, all things you do on your own. However, now chat rooms on-line were my only connection to people that were not related to me or being paid to be with me. I felt like I was totally isolated from people my own age. Chat rooms were my one and only connection to people anywhere near my age. That's most likely another reason I was so smitten by Julie. She was roughly my age, she was a babe, she understood where I was coming from, if you know what I mean, and she was full of life. But damn, she's married!

Enough of Julie, for now. I read a lot, mostly books. I read Tom Clancy, John Grisham, and Michael Crighton, all those "guy" books. I also read a lot magazines. Macintosh Computer magazines. I had become a total computer nerd. I didn't really care. I mean I had no social life and I was living at home with my parents.

When I wasn't reading, using my computer, or reading about my computer, I was doing my therapy, or at least something…anything, to get my life back. The most important thing for me at the time was being able to put my contacts in, I don't really know why it was such a big deal for me, but it was. I guess I didn't feel like a "stud" with my glasses on. I had been wearing contacts since junior high school and felt very self-conscious without them in. I didn't think girls would think I was a babe if I had my glasses on. Plus, I wanted Julie to see me with my contacts in. I thought, *Maybe her marriage is on the rocks, and I'll be there.* I told you I was arrogant.

This whole episode of the bike crash, being in the hospital for three and a half months, being in a wheelchair, not being able speak very clearly, having to wear my glasses again, and having to live at home with my parents, absolutely demolished my self-esteem. In my entire life, I had never had low self-esteem until now. Now it was so low, I would have to stand on a nickel to pee on a dime.

I felt I would have a little better self-esteem if I could get my contacts in and not have to wear glasses. Then one day, I got them in. It was almost orgasmic! It was such a relief! Glasses really are a pain in the ass. They get dirty, they slide down your nose, they fall off, and you can't just put t-shirts or sweaters on, or take them off. You always worry about your glasses. Now, a huge burden felt like it was gone, not to mention how much better I perceived myself. I had a minuscule amount of confidence back. Social confidence, that is.

I actually couldn't wait to go to the hospital for therapy because Julie would see me without my glasses. I didn't really care if she was married, she was just so cute. So I went to therapy and saw Julie, and she saw me…no sparks flew or anything like that, I just felt better about myself.

I continued going to therapy for a few more months. I had gotten to the point where I could do my therapeutic exercises and/or activities without supervision. I was given a list of exercises and activities to do, and I would just go to the therapy department, when it was convenient for me, and do them.

CHAPTER 24

At this point in my saga, I could drive. That too, took a lot of work. I started by driving an old Willy's jeep my dad has. It is pretty indestructible. It didn't go very fast and was very decrepit. I figured if I hit a tree, the tree would come out worse than the jeep. It is a manual transmission so I had to shift, but it didn't move very fast so I rarely even got to third gear. It didn't have power steering and the brakes required a lot of force, so driving it was a pretty good workout. I would drive it to the only store in Angwin and then drive back. I can't accurately describe that freedom.

I had spent three and a half months in a hospital, where I couldn't do anything without someone else's help. I was living at home where I could not go anywhere without someone taking and bringing me back. I was a TBI teenager who couldn't drive yet. I really wanted to drive. I did have a drivers license, however it was invalid. When a hospital gets a patient with a head injury, they are required by law to notify the DMV. The DMV was notified of me and revoked my license. I, of course, wanted it back. I wanted my life back. I could wear my contacts now, so things were looking up. Next on my list was a driver's license.

Prior to my accident I had a Nissan Sentra. It was getting old and beat-up so I wanted a new car. I had considered moving back home, while I was working, in order to save money to buy a new car. I really wanted a Toyota 4Runner. It would be a great car for going to places to mountain bike or rock climb, and you could sleep in it if you couldn't find a camping spot. I figured it was the perfect vehicle for me, so much so, that I was going to willingly put myself in the situation I was now forced into; that is living at home, in order to save enough money to buy a 4Runner. There was one difference, I would be working, so I wouldn't be home much and when I wasn't working I'd be mountain biking.

Enter the part of me that is a vindictive jerk, and even more so post TBI. I had my Dad get a lawyer because I was going to sue the lady who hit me. My father was a school teacher for thirty some odd years and it just so happened a kid he had in the fifth grade, Paul, turned out to be a lawyer in Napa. My father contacted him to see what could be done.

I'll make a long story short. It was determined to be in my best interest to settle out of court. The reason being the accident was partially my fault. It was dusk, I didn't have bike light or any reflectors, and I was speeding. The speed limit on the hill I was riding down is 35 MPH. It was determined I was doing between 40 and 50 MPH. I've ridden down that hill a number of times, and I was probably going closer to, if not over, 50 MPH.

As I mentioned before, the streetlight was not working and there was a question as to how long it had not been working. Was the length of time it had been non-operational acceptable by law? Also, it was not possible to know if the woman driving the car had her directional on at the time of the crash, or had simply put it on after the crash.

So essentially, the insurance company of the woman driving the car said, "O.K. Here is X amount of money. Take it and the case is closed." My lawyer advised me to take it, because if I went to court, I could have gotten nothing.

CHAPTER 25

So now I had, what I considered, a lot of money. The first thing I did was go to a bank. I already had a checking account and a Money Market Account (MMA). I put a fair percentage of the money in the MMA, a little bit in my checking account, but the majority went into a CD and a mutual fund. Previous to my accident, I had spent a fair amount of time learning what to do with the money I earned. I felt I had put that knowledge to pretty good use.

So now, I had some money, and just felt better about the whole thing. During the lawsuit I had a chance to look at a report of the assets of the lady who hit me and her husband. They really didn't have squat! It did, however, make me feel better. I can't say I don't have hard feelings toward the woman and I can't say that I have forgiven her. However, I won't hunt her down and kill her, I wouldn't hit her if I saw her, I wouldn't even call her names if I was faced with her. I certainly wouldn't invite her over for dinner, but I wouldn't mind talking with her.

Back to therapy. Up to now I had been basically relegated to a wheelchair to get around. Now, however, with the hours and hours of therapy and hard work, I could walk around with a walker. This reminds me of an amusing story. At this time, my grandmother was alive but in poor health. She required a walker also to get around. Now, having to use a walker like an old lady was a huge blow to my ego. But I figured, *Oh, what the hell it's better than a wheelchair*. One day I was out walking, with my walker around the yard. I got to thinking that the next time I saw my Grandmother I would challenge her to a race. For some reason that just struck me as hilarious. It was the first time since I moved back home, that I had truly just laughed and I couldn't stop. My Grandmothers name was Marion, so I named my walker Marion.

One thing I've learned through this whole TBI ordeal is that laughter truly is the best medicine. Laughter can't fix a broken bone or stop a bleeding wound but it can make you feel happy, relaxed, and just plain good. If you're are in a good mood; you are inclined do your therapy better and more often, you try things and don't get frustrated as easily, you just keep trying until you succeed. For me, if I had a good laugh, life just seemed better and I was in a good mood and therefore willing to work harder at repairing myself from my crash. So I tried to keep things "light." I would try to make a joke about anything I could. If I hadn't done that I would have been a lot more depressed than I was, and I was pretty depressed. I watched funny TV shows. I read funny books. I saw funny movies. I read the comics in the paper, except Family Circle. I tried to immerse myself in comedy every chance I got, otherwise I couldn't have put up with my life anymore. I just couldn't take it.

I could walk around pretty well with a walker and even go short distances, on flat ground without a walker. I could put my contact lenses in, and so a very small bit of self-esteem came back to me. I was actually looking forward to going to therapy at the hospital, mainly so I could see Julie. I was TBI teenager and so, like all teenagers, my hormones were going absolutely nuts!

CHAPTER 26

Speech. I never really thought much about my speech. I don't think anyone thinks about their speech, unless it becomes a problem. My speech was a problem. At first, I just couldn't make all the proper sounds. I had speech therapy while I was still at The Queen of the Valley Hospital. I had speech therapy at my house when I first got out of the hospital. Then I had speech therapy at Pacific Union College (PUC). The speech therapist that worked with me at home, taught at PUC also and so eventually my therapy sessions were held there. PUC is located a couple of miles from my parents house.

The speech therapists name was Jennifer. I liked her. She was pretty cool. One problem with my speech was my inability to make the proper sounds. I had a doctor named Dr. Crutcher, however, I couldn't say Crutcher. I would always say "Cratcher." It was really weird and extremely frustrating. Jennifer worked with me a lot to say "Crutcher" instead of "Cratcher."

When I first started speech therapy at PUC, my mother drove there and then drove me home when I was done. The sessions were about an hour long. I liked going to PUC for therapy because it is a college and colleges have women. I just wanted to look at them because I was not going to talk with any of them.

PUC is less than a mile, as the crow flies, from my house. There is a wilderness trail that one can take from near my house to near the campus. At this point, as a result of all therapy, hard work, and the passage of time, I could walk on my own. So I decided I would benefit from walking to speech therapy, plus I didn't like all the college students seeing me being driven around by my Mom.

The first day I walked to speech therapy on the wilderness trail, I was scared shitless! What should have taken fifteen to twenty minutes took an hour. That was because I had to figure out ways to get around logs, rocks, branches, holes, and other obstacles on a wilderness trail. Fortunately, I had planned for this, and so left for my speech therapy more than an hour early. I could walk to PUC but was to out of shape to make the round trip, so my Mom would bring me home.

Angwin is a small town. There is the university and there is a store. I would walk to speech therapy and then rest for about an hour. Well my mouth wouldn't rest, but the rest of me would. When my therapy was over, I would walk across campus, across the street, and to the store, which had a pay phone. I would call my Mom and she would come pick me up. I really looked forward to my speech therapy. I could walk on the wilderness trail, which I'm sure was good therapy. I would have speech therapy, which was making my speech better, which was a good thing. I got to walk across campus and look at all the girls. Another bonus was that PUC is on a hill, so consequently there are a lot of stairs. Walking up and down stairs was very therapeutic for me. It was good for balance and coordination. I don't remember how long I had speech therapy there, but it was until my insurance ran out.

Now is as good as any time as any to tell about my insurance. I had Blue Cross from when I worked for Flora Springs Wine Co. It was very good. I didn't see any of my hospital bills, but I heard the figures $30,000 and $40,000 a couple of times, of which I owed $0.00. Flora Springs Wine Co. kept me on their insurance policy for a couple of years after the accident, and I can't stress enough how wonderful that was. I had a lot worries, stress, and problems, but one I did not have was worrying about hospital bills. I can only imagine how awful it must be to be in a terrible car accident, or something, and not have health insurance. If I hadn't had any, I would probably have to live in some sort of "home" because I couldn't take care of myself and the insurance company was tired of paying hospital bills. I said it before, and I'll say it again: Dr. Bodor, Tex, Honeydew Chic, and probably a few others, most likely saved my life by convincing the insurance company that I should go into Acute Rehabilitation. They saved my life because I would have found a way to commit suicide had I been living in some sort of "home." The insurance did eventually stop paying for my speech therapy. After all my speech therapy, I could make all the correct sounds. I could say, "Crutcher" instead of, "Cratcher." One problem I did have, and still have to this day, is regulating the speed at which I talk. I just can't seem to regulate the speed of my mouth and tongue. As a result, I'm extremely difficult to understand. If I concentrate really hard, I can speak slowly and clearly, but it requires an incredible amount of thought.

I firmly believe that because my speech is rough, slurred, and that I'm hard to understand has caused people to view me as, shall we say, less than intelligent. I think people hear me speak and think I'm a "retard.," no offense to anyone. I really think speech plays a vital role in one's ability, or inability, to get a job.

One thing I did to try and regulate my speech speed was to sing some songs. My brother-in-law had a CD by the band Alice In Chains. This CD was designed to play on a computer. When the CD was played on my computer, the lyrics would be displayed. It wasn't fast music at all, so by reading and singing the lyrics in time with band, I was practicing regulating my speed. It was very difficult. I could sing the entire song before the first verse was completed, of course you couldn't understand a word I said. My speech was really getting me down.

CHAPTER 27

I mentioned Dr. Green before. He was the psychologist, or "shrink", I had seen in Acute Rehab. Upon being released from the hospital, I had to have a psychologist. Dr. Green recommended a Dr. Tim Berry, who also happened to be his business partner.

The first session I had with Dr. Tim Berry, I cried. Which I guess was the desired effect of his questions. I wasn't lying on a couch, or anything, just sitting in a nice comfortable chair. I saw Dr. Berry three times per week at first, then down to once a week. My insurance covered this, which was essential. Those shrinks charge a boatload and my settlement with the insurance company was a dinghyload. I liked going to see Dr. Berry, at first. I could, and would, tell him anything. I totally trusted him. I assume that is pretty imperative for a psychologist; to gain the trust of the patient. Well, he had gained mine.

One day, I just came in and simply said I was going to kill myself. Dr. Berry asked for my car keys and then asked me why. He remained totally calm didn't get riled-up or panicked, anything like that. He asked how I was going to commit suicide. I hadn't actually figured that out yet, so I just told him I was going to jump in front of a big truck. That would have been nearly impossible because I could barely walk, let alone jump in front of a truck. He then asked why I was going to kill myself. I thought, *Well, duh. Because my life totally sucks.* He then asked me to be specific about how my life sucked. To make a long story short, I realized that my life could actually be worse and that I had gotten better and had hope of continuing to get better. He wouldn't, however, give my car keys back, I guess because I was still a suicide risk. Therefore, I couldn't get home and my brother-in-law had to come pick me up. I had to spend the night at he and my sisters house. Which was fine.

The next day, I went home and probably had some sort of therapy that day. I don't remember exactly when I saw Dr. Berry again, but I wasn't suicidal. In fact, I was relatively "happy." I could get around without my wheelchair, I saw Julie a couple of times a week, (I was totally smitten) plus I thought I was totally rich, from my settlement with the insurance company. Life was good...I thought.

I called my sessions with Dr. Berry "thought therapy" because that is what they were. I got so I didn't think about what I'd lost, which was everything, but about what I still had, which wasn't much. I was diagnosed with Post Traumatic Stress Disorder or Syndrome, I don't remember the correct name. I guess my brain injury was the "traumatic stress" in my current mental state. However, I think a better name for my condition would have been Post Traumatic Depression Disorder, because I was extremely depressed. After a while, I don't remember how long, I was down to just one session of "thought therapy" per week. I had gotten to the point where I enjoyed talking with Dr. Berry, I could tell him anything, as I totally trusted him. Plus he was a guy, and 99% of the people I had any contact with were women. Not that I didn't like any of those women, it was just nice to talk with a guy, besides my Dad or the occasional time I worked and talked with the therapist Ron. I'm telling you though, I was kicking myself for not majoring in psychology in college. If it hadn't been for my insurance, through Flora Springs, I would have had to see another psychologist to deal with paying those shrink bills.

Later in my recovery, I did, thankfully, have another male therapist, Michael, who was younger than me. I had known of

Michael since I was in the 5th grade, since he lived near me, but I never knew him personally, until now. He turned out to be a pretty cool guy, even if it was to have therapy with.

Now is as good as time as any to tell of one seemingly miniscule event, but which, in fact, was huge in my mental well being. I've stated before that I had to sit down and "pee like a girl," and that it was a huge blow to my self-esteem. My brother-in-law is a photographer. He was taking pictures for Peter Micheal Winery. He wanted to take some pictures of the vineyards on the bottom of Mt. St. Helena. He asked if I wanted to go along for the ride. I did. So we went. We got to the vineyards, which are on the side and bottom of the mountain and surrounded by foliage. My brother-in-law stopped the truck because he had to take a pee, so did I. He got out and found a tree, so did I. I was kind of freaking out because there was no place to sit. I didn't really know what to do. Now, I've always been a very proud guy, I'm sure some people would say too proud. I really didn't want to ask my brother-in-law for help, so I just undid my pants, stood by the tree, and took a wiz. I couldn't believe it! I actually did it. Just stood there and took a pee. It was the first time I had felt like any sort of man since my accident. It's a good thing I took my "maiden voyage" outdoors because my balance wasn't very good and therefore my "aim" was atrocious. I'll never forget that day and am forever indebted to my brother-in-law for taking me. It was just such an ordinary thing to do. My depression was minutely less after that day.

CHAPTER 28

At this point, I wasn't confined to a wheelchair. I can't even begin to express what a difference that made. I did, however, need a walker. I felt like an old lady when I used my walker. Walking with a walker is harder than you might think. You have to pick it up, move it forward, and then move yourself forward. This sounds pretty simple and straight forward and it is, unless you've had a brain injury. Then it becomes pretty difficult!

My right deltoid, and therefore shoulder, was shot to hell and not to helpful in moving Marion forward. My balance was at best questionable and so my arms would get extremely tired from holding myself up with Marion. Moving my feet forward was no small task, either. But hey, I was out of the wheelchair so it was all worth it.

I remember my big expedition was getting the mail. The mailbox is across the street, which is a couple hundred feet from the house. I would look forward to the mail coming so that I could venture out and get it. Of course the only thing I ever got were bills. Well no, not really, I subscribed to a couple of Macintosh magazines, and so would get those. I remember I couldn't hold on to Marion and all the mail at the same time. So, whenever I went out to get the mail, I would bring a little bag with handles, I could put the mail in the bag, hold on to the bag's handles, hold on to Marion, and eventually get back in the house. I must have been quite a site. A young, adult male, with a walker, carrying a little bag with handles, getting the mail, and then putting the mail in the little bag. This truly was an expedition for me. I don't remember how long it would take, but it was quite awhile. I would be so worn out after this expedition, I couldn't even use my computer.

This expedition eventually became just a trip out to the mailbox, and I needed an expedition. So I decided I was going to go around the block with Marion. It wasn't a typical city block. It was much larger. Basically it was just the shortest round trip I could take. I thought about doing this for days before I actually attempted it. I started mentally preparing myself the night before the day I was going to do it. When the day came, I was very excited but a little scared. Since my "birth" on Sept. 15, 1995, the farthest away from people I could get was going out to the mailbox. Now I was going to embark on a trip that, relative to anything I had done since my TBI birth, was like walking across the United States. I'm sure my Mom was more scared than I was, and I was more determined than scared.

So, in the early afternoon, I got all warmly dressed, grabbed Marion, and embarked on my adventure. It was extremely slow going. At the time, I couldn't put one foot in front of the other. I would always start stepping forward with my right foot. However, I could only bring my left foot even with my right foot. I couldn't put my left foot in front of my right foot. I have no idea why.

Angwin is located on the top of Howell Mountain, so there aren't any flat streets. I was on a downward sloping street and was approximately halfway around the block, and getting pretty tired. I don't know what or how exactly this happened but I fell over the front of my walker and was laying in the street. Angwin is a small town and it was a weekday, so there was no traffic. I remember lying in the street and thinking, *Okay, Now what the hell do I do?* I crawled over to Marion and managed to pull and push myself upright. This whole process took a good fifteen to twenty minutes, but I was ready to continue on my journey. I continued on until I was three quarters of the way around the block when my Dad drove up and said, "Your mother was getting worried and told me to look for you." I was very glad to see him, as I was extremely tired and the final street on my expedition started out with a steep downhill and ended with a steep uphill. I don't think I would have made it. I probably would fallen over and hurt myself or I would have gotten too tired, just quit, and waited for someone to come looking for me.

So, my dad took me home and I was just tired. My toast was more than popped; I was burnt toast. I was frustrated, too, because I hadn't actually completed my "journey." It was still pretty significant, but I felt I didn't complete it without some help. I don't know if it's a guy thing, or just me, but I hate it when I start something and don't finish it. Fortunately, I was too tired to think about it much, so I just sat on the couch and watched TV.

Speaking of TV, prior to my accident, when I was living alone, and working, I didn't own a TV. I just didn't care about any of the stuff that was on TV, with one exception: sports. I would go to my parent's house, where I now lived, to watch the San Francisco 49ers or the San Francisco Giants, but that was it. Now, however, TV was a big part of my life. If I wasn't doing some sort of therapy or using my computer, I was watching TV. I didn't watch any of those Ricki Lake type shows or soap operas, but I'd watch just about anything else. My parents don't have cable or a satellite dish, just an antennae. They only get about nine or ten channels and I watched them all. I then remembered why I didn't own a TV before: there is too much crap on TV. It didn't take long for me to get pretty disgusted with TV. So I took up reading. I read a lot of books, I still do.

CHAPTER 29

I had, from my settlement, what I considered a lot of money. What's the first thing I bought? A new bicycle. I don't really know why, I just wanted a new bike. The bike I crashed on looked O.K., except for the front rim, which was pretty much destroyed, but I was afraid of hairline fractures, or something, in the frame. I didn't want to be riding the bike ad have it fall apart, so I figured I needed a new bicycle. Thankfully, no one discouraged me from buying it because it turned out to be incredibly motivating. I could barely walk at the time, was still using Marion on occasion, and still going to therapy, but having a new bike just made me even more determined to ride it.

It was a nice bike. The nicest bike I had ever owned and I wanted to ride it, but that was pretty much out of the question. My balance was barely good enough to walk, let alone ride a bike. So I got a trainer to attach the bicycle to. I'm not a fitness nut, or anything, I just liked physical exercise. Prior to my accident, I discovered that I would always feel better about life in general after riding my bike. So now, I hoped to get the same result, even though the bike was attached to a trainer. I guess I'm addicted to adrenaline.

There was one problem, however. I couldn't put my shoes on without help. My bicycle shoes fit pretty tight, and I just couldn't pull, or push, them on. Probably because the necessary muscles had atrophied. Whenever I wanted to ride my bike on the trainer I would have to have my Mom help me put my shoes on. That doesn't do much for your self-esteem. I didn't really care though, because I was going to ride my nice, new bicycle. It is a red, Salsa La Raza with nice Shimano components.

When I first started riding the bike, I did it indoors in front of the TV. I would watch/listen to my Metallica videotapes. I don't really remember how long I rode for, probably only a half an hour or so. Even watching something on TV I would just get totally bored. I don't remember ever stopping because I was tired, just because I was bored. It did make me feel alive again. I had previously considered myself "dead." In a way, I was. Every aspect of my life had been lost or changed. It was as if someone put my life in a bag, shook it all up, and through it out on the ground. Riding a bicycle, even if it was hooked up to a trainer, was the first "piece" of my life I had picked-up on my own, even if I couldn't get my shoes on. Plus, I take great pride in my physique. Being in the hospital for three and a half months, eating hospital food, then living at home, being confined to a wheelchair, and basically just sitting down all the time was making me a little rotund. I didn't like that. Now, I could at least pedal a bicycle and work-up a sweat. Once again, I was minutely less depressed, but I was still incredibly depressed.

I felt I was on my way back, just because I could "ride" a bike. When I started riding with the trainer I was indoors. I like the outdoors. So as soon as the weather got semi-warm, my whole bicycle contraption was moved out onto the lawn. I could walk out to my bike, get on, and "ride" for an hour or so. I could hear the birds, watch squirrels, watch the dogs, and just breath fresh air. Life was good, but not great.

Riding my bike on the trainer, outside, just made me even more determined to ride my bike again, without the trainer. I had this nice, new road bicycle, but I also had a well-used mountain bike. Mountain bikes aren't built for speed, like road bicycles are. Therefore, the angles of the frame, handlebars, etc. allow the bicycle rider to be in more natural sitting position. More importantly though, I think, is mountain bikes have fatter tires. A mountain bike is much more forgiving when it comes to balancing, and I needed a lot of forgiveness.

My first obstacle was just getting on the bike. I needed my brother-in-laws help, and a wooden fence, but I got on my mountain bike. I'm pretty sure all I did was just sit on the bike seat, I may have pedaled backwards, but I certainly didn't go anywhere. This was a big deal to me! I was actually on a bicycle again! Maybe I could ride one again...maybe. They say once you learn to ride a bike, you never forget. Well, if you've had a TBI that is not true. I forgot. I had no clue, not to mention any sense of balance.

I was not physically a little kid who could try to ride a bike for hours on end and just get skinned knees and elbows. I was a grown man and in terrible physical condition. I couldn't just hop on my bike, pedal once or twice, fall over, and start all over again. That's how I learned the first time.

I would get on my mountain bike, which was no small task, my brother-in-law would hold on to the seat post, so I wouldn't fall over, and I would pedal and "ride" my bike, with him running alongside me holding the seat post. One day, my brother-in-law, Olaf, was holding on to my seat and I started to ride around the block. Olaf had to hold to my bike so he was running along side me. He wasn't wearing tennis shoes, or anything even close, and he had pants on. I don't care how slowly one pedals a bike, if they pedal at all, they are still going to go faster than someone on foot. Olaf is 6' 8" tall and so has very long legs, but I couldn't believe he could stay with me. It was blowing my mind. Not only that he could do it, but that he *was* doing it. Everything went fine until the final little hill up to the house. Well, it wasn't a little hill to me, it was Mt. Everest. My legs gave out about a quarter of the way up, and I fell over. I had to walk the rest of the way home, but that's key. I could walk, so I didn't really care about not making it all the way on my bike.

CHAPTER 30

Enter Mike. When I had my accident I stupidly had no ID. So no one knew who I was. The authorities started asking around if anyone knew a young blonde male with a Bianchi road bicycle. Someone suggested calling Mike, who owned Palisade's bike shop in Calistoga. Mike said he knew who it was. Bianchi bicycles aren't very common around these parts. So Mike called my sister, she called my mom and all hell broke loose. They had to drive to the Queen of the Valley Hospital and identify me. This whole process took some time. It was now Saturday and I had crashed on Friday.

Jump ahead. Mike, in his store, has a mountain bike for rent that is a tandem. Mike would loan this bike to Olaf, and he and I would ride the tandem. The best part of it was I didn't really have to balance the bicycle, Olaf did that. All I did was sit on the bike and pedal. That sounds a lot easier than it actually was. Sitting on a small seat while it, and I, was moving, was a pretty big challenge for me. I had never actually seen my knuckles turn white from gripping something so hard, but they certainly did when I was riding on the tandem bicycle.

At first we stayed on paved roads. After I became somewhat comfortable on the bike, and my knuckles regained some color, we went off-road. Nothing to rough, just dirt roads. It just so happened that these dirt roads were part of the area in which I had done the majority of my mountain biking. There is also a good NORBA race there, The Napa Valley Dirt Classic, which I had raced in a few times previous to my crash. Being back on at least part of the racecourse made me really want to ride again. I previously figured I would never see this area again, let alone ride on it.

My brother-in-law and I rode the tandem mountain bike a number of times. I was becoming pretty comfortable riding it, so tried to imagine riding solo, i.e. having to balance the bike myself. I don't know if it helped but it made me feel like I was doing something to get my life back. I would also attempt to ride my mountain bike solo but I would always crash. I was kicking myself for not having bought stock in Bactine or Band-Aid. I'd rival Bill Gates in wealth now, if I had. I also attached my mountain bike to the trainer, out on the lawn. I didn't think it was possible, but I was now even more determined to ride my bike again!

Somewhere along here I was able to ride my bike solo; no help getting my shoes on, no help getting on or off the bike, no help riding it. I just remember that it was the first time, since my crash, that I was glad to be alive. I'm not kidding. Before, I didn't really care if I lived or died. I don't know why that was the case. I wasn't a pro bicyclist or anything even close. However, now, I figured I had "salvaged" one small piece of my formerly very happy existence.

I do remember the first time I was able to ride my new Salsa road bicycle. I did not need any human help to get on my bike. I did need a fence or garage door to lean-on while I got on. Just getting on the bike was a major undertaking and took quite a few minutes. The first time I rode I started in one of the absolute worst gears I could have been in. I neglected to look at that before I started. I was in one of the biggest gears on the bicycle. What that means is I was in one of the gears for going fast. It was sort of like starting out driving a fast sports car in fifth gear. Once I got on the bike and started pedaling, I realized my mistake. However, me being me, and the fact that it so much work just to get on the bike, I figured I would just muscle it out. Big mistake. My bicycle riding muscles had recovered somewhat but not enough to begin in the big gear I was in. I pedaled three or four times, at most, and was going way to fast. My brain didn't have the organization yet to just put on the brakes and slow down, so I just kept going. I went out the driveway, across the street, and nailed an outdoor lamp by the neighbor's driveway. The lamp broke in half and I was in major pain. My maiden voyage on my new Salsa had gone about 30-40 yards. I wasn't hurt. Just a couple nasty bruises. To this day, I have yet to figure how I got them. They were on the inside of each of my thighs, near the family jewels, and they were about six to eight inches long, and boy did they hurt. I was not really black and blue there, it was mostly black. It was ugly. I didn't really care though, because I had ridden the bike totally solo.

I kept thinking, *The only thing I did wrong was start in the wrong gear. That's easily correctable.* I can be a stubborn S.O.B. if I want to, and riding my new Salsa bicycle made me want to be. I was going to ride that bike if it was the last thing I did! So I took a couple days off, to heal, and I just thought about riding the bike. I mentally went through *every* little aspect of riding my bike. From what gear to start in, what my route would be, what I should eat, to actually imagining I was riding the bike.

The day came for me to ride my Salsa again. I got all prepared for my ride, which took quite awhile. I made sure I was in a smaller, slower, gear and got on the bike. I used the garage door as a "bicycle mounting aid." That was a bit of a reality check for me and took away a little confidence, but not enough to make me abort my mission, which was to ride my shiny, new, bright red Salsa. I started off, at a manageable speed this time, went past my neighbors broken garden light and regained some confidence.

I just remember it felt so...so...good to be riding again. It felt so good, that I was going places I probably shouldn't be going. My legs were much stronger than I had hoped, probably as a result of riding the trainer so much. I was riding up hills that I really had no idea that I would be able to ride up. Of course, if you ride uphill you have to ride downhill. I just kept going. I figured I would ride to the local grocery store, and if I was too tired to ride back home, I would call. I never made it to the store.

I was riding for the first time with a mirror attached to my helmet, as I was a little paranoid of cars. I remember that I was getting used to looking in the mirror while riding, which was rather strange. My legs were feeling like wet noodles because they had been inactive for so long and I was getting winded. The last thing I remember is I was going down a pretty steep hill, I was wobbling on my bike, and I was trying to make use of my "rear-view mirror." The next thing I know, there is a pretty cute chic is asking me my name, where I live, where I am. There were a couple of guys there busily doing something, but I don't know exactly what. It turns out, they were putting me on a stretcher. Then I was put into an ambulance, and driven to the St. Hospital and Health Center emergency room. While riding in the ambulance it dawned on me that I must have been in another bicycle crash. I hoped no cars were involved. I remember thinking; *This is pretty cool, being in an ambulance with a cute EMT.* I didn't remember my first trip in an ambulance, so this was new to me.

When we arrived in the emergency room, I was rushed into a room, where I was expecting to see all kinds of activity, but my expectations were wrong. It was dead, pun intended. I laid there on the stretcher, or whatever it was, for what seemed like an eternity. All I remember is a lady asking me if there was someone they could call. I said you can call my Mom but she'll freak out. The nurse said she would break it to her gently. Next thing I knew, my mom and dad were at the hospital.

I wasn't in the hospital for very long. Just enough time for some tests and X-rays. I was released about dinnertime, my Mom was in no mood to cook, and so we went out to dinner. The test results were mostly negative. I received a concussion, but that is all. Nothing broken. No brain injury, a scrape or two, but nothing more serious. I did, however, decide to quit riding my bike...for awhile.

CHAPTER 31

I'm pretty sure I had technically turned twenty-six years old at this point. In reality I was still a TBI teenager. Like the first time I was a teenager, I wanted to drive. Problem was: A) I didn't have a car, and B) I didn't have a valid driver's license. From what I understand, doctors, or hospitals, are required to notify the Department of Motor Vehicles (DMV) if a patient has had a head injury, and I certainly had. My driver's license was invalid. Plus, I couldn't drive anyway, as I had forgotten how and my right shoulder would not cooperate. My shoulder seemed to have a mind of its own and refused to do what I told it. It was very annoying.

I had to learn to drive again. My dad has an old Willys Jeep that he uses for hunting. It's pretty well thrashed, but it runs. It's a manual transmission but it only has three gears and is pretty easy to shift. I figured I could hit a tree at top speed and no one would know it. So I decided I would relearn to drive in the jeep. So I did. At first I just backed-up and went forward a couple of times. It was a hell of a lot harder than it sounds. I could not comprehend how I, or anyone, could actually have their foot do one thing, (depress the clutch) while their hand did something completely different, (shift gears). It was just beyond me. But I figured it out pretty fast. It didn't take long for me to get antsy and want to actually drive on a road.

I started out just going around our block. After I did that a couple of times, I was ready to tackle the epic journey of driving the crummy ol' jeep to the "store", which was only about two miles away, but it was world's away for me.

I had tried to avoid the "store" in Angwin since I was about fifteen, but now it was the big city to me. There were people there that weren't doctors, nurses, therapists, or family members. It was totally foreign to me, but I thought it was great. I drove to the store a few times and then figured it was time to get serious about obtaining a driver's license.

CHAPTER 32

E veryone agreed. It was time to *legally* get ready to drive. The first step was to take driving lessons. My parents contacted the North Bay Driving School and arranged lessons for me. The driving instructor came to my house a couple of days later and took me out for a lesson. That's the good news. As soon as the instructor arrived at my house, things went downhill.

The instructor was an old, fuddy-duddy guy. The car I was going to use was all set up for people with any number of different handicaps. I could not get over all switches, levers, peddles, handles and other paraphernalia that I'd never seen before in a car. I didn't have much choice, however, so I just got in the car. I began driving, I was nervous as hell, and the instructor just kept asking me driving questions. I could not do *anything* correctly. I either slowed too fast or not fast enough. I was too close to the car in front of me, or I should get closer. I took corners to fast and/or wide, or not fast and/or wide enough. No matter what I did, it wasn't the proper or best way. It gets better, or worse, in my opinion. Towards the end of the first lesson, we passed a speed limit sign, nothing wrong or unusual about that. The instructor asked me what the sign meant. I thought he was kidding but he wasn't. I said, "You can't drive faster than the sign says." He said, "Yes, but there is more to it." I said, "It's illegal to drive over the speed limit and you could get a ticket." He said, "Yes, but what else?" I said, "Uuhhh…you *really* can't drive over the speed limit." He said, "Yes, but there is something else. Most people don't get it." I racked my brain, but I could not think of what else a speed limit sign meant. I thought, *Oh boy, here we go. I'll find out there's another part of my brain that is all screwed up.* For the life of me, I could not think of the answer. I said, "I don't know what else it means." The instructor said, "Well, you can't go faster than the sign says, but you can any speed *up to* what the sign says." I almost stopped the car, got out, and punched him. I said, "Ohh, okay." I was thinking, however, *He's wrong. I could not drive on a highway at 5 MPH and not get pulled over by a cop. Driving that slow would probably cause a crash.* That was near the end of my lesson, and the remaining few minutes were bearable.

At the same time I was taking my driving lessons, I was also receiving speech therapy. I basically had to learn to speak all over again. I had the same frustrations with speech as I had with tying my shoe. That being, I knew that I knew how to talk, but when I spoke, it just came out gibberish. My main problem was I spoke to fast. One result of my brain injury was that I could not regulate the speed with which I spoke. My tongue, lips, and whatever else is used for speech, seemed to have a life of their own.

Another problem was my mouth would get really tired. I guess the mouth muscles, here is that word again, had atrophied. I did mouth and tongue exercises at home and my whole face would just be worn out.

One day, at speech therapy after my driving "lesson", I was complaining about the driving instructor to my speech therapist. I don't remember the specifics, but my speech therapist called my driving instructor. He said that I was doing fine, that speech therapy was very important, and I should continue having it. At my next speech therapy session, the therapist related the story to me. At the end of the story she said that he was, "just a fuddy-duddy."

Eventually, I could say "Crutcher" instead of "Cratcher." My driving lessons were also concluded. Zippity-doo-da! Now I needed to take the written portion test. I was to take the written portion of the drivers test in Santa Rosa, CA. My mother had to drive me to Santa Rosa to take the test, so we got in the car and off we went.

Talk about a miserable déjà vu! I did not like being a teenager the first time. I thought it was pretty lame, but everyone has to be one at some point. Now I was doing it all over again! My mom, or dad, had to drive me around because I couldn't drive, just like being a teenager. I was going through the DMV bullshit again, just like I did when I was a teenager. I was a TBI teenager, which turned out to be a hell of a lot worse, or harder, than just being a regular teenager.

I arrived at the DMV in Santa Rosa and took the written portion of the test. I had to take it twice before I passed, but I passed. Now I had to take the driving portion of the test.

Before I get to that, however, I'll share with the reader one reason I was so determined to get my drivers license. When I was working at Flora Springs Winery, I was driving an old, beat-up Nissan Sentra. I would drive to mountain bike races and also to places where I could go rock climbing. A Nissan Sentra was not the ideal vehicle for those endeavors.

I have just remembered that the story I'm about to relate, took place before I had driving lessons with the North Bay Driving School. I will also remind the reader that the decision I should get a 4Runner took place *before* my bicycle crash.

Now, I have forgotten the exact sequence of events here, only because it's been a few years not because my memory has been diminished from my brain injury. I've been told repeatedly that my memory has been affected and I'll have trouble remembering stuff, but that's another story.

I wanted a Toyota 4Runner. Problem was, I did not have a valid driver's license so I could not even go to a dealership to drool over one. At the time, my sister, Stephanie, was going through a divorce. She was living at home, the same time I was. Anyhow, right before Christmas, December 23, 1996 to be exact, she was going to take me to a Toyota dealership in Santa Rosa, after she returned from Christmas shopping. I watched the clock all day, as the seconds crawled by, until Stephanie returned home. Finally, after what seemed an eternity, Stephanie returned home from Santa Rosa.

I said, "When do you want to go to Santa Rosa?" I was thinking she would say, "After dinner." But no….she said that she did not want to go back to Santa Rosa. She just came from there. She will go with me some other day. Well, I lost it. All the frustration, which was a hell of a lot, that I'd stored up since September 15, 1995, just spilled out. I went to my fathers gun cabinet and took out a rifle, or maybe a shotgun, I don't remember which. However, either one would have accomplished the desired result. I won't bother explaining what that was. I am not exactly certain why I wanted that result right then. Buying a 4Runner, or any car for that matter, wasn't that important to me. I think it symbolized something because I had wanted a 4Runner prior to my crash and now, with all that happened, I could get one, if it weren't for my tired sister. Maybe it symbolized that I had recovered and could live somewhat of a "normal" life. Whatever it symbolized, it wasn't going to happen then and I was not happy.

So I had the rifle and was going to use it on myself, I figured I probably wouldn't miss. This is when another one of my brother-in-laws, Tom, saved me. He offered to take me to Santa Rosa right then and there, if I let go of the gun. So I did. I got my checkbook and off we went. We did not really know where we were going, so we had to stop and ask where the "auto row" was.

CHAPTER 33

We arrived at the Toyota dealership, and went straight inside. We were asked if we needed some help, and I said, "I want to buy a 4Runner." The dealer said, "O.K. We have....." I told him I want this, that, and the other thing and he showed me a 4Runner that met my desires.

After pulling out a shotgun, threatening to blow my brains out, and having Tom drive me to Santa Rosa, all because I wasn't going to get a 4Runner right then; made it so I couldn't exactly change my mind and go home without a 4Runner. In addition I hate car salesman, and shopping in general, so I just said, "O.K. I'll take that one." It took about ten minutes. Then I had to actually *buy* the 4Runner. That took considerably longer.

When the dealer asked me how I wanted to purchase the 4Runner, I asked him if I could just write a check. I did not want to deal with the hassles of a lease, or payments, or anything like that, I just wanted my new SUV. I had never bought a car before and I was going through all kinds of emotional, physical and mental crap. Therefore, I just wanted to keep it simple.

The dealer's eyes got big and he told me he would have to call my bank. He called my bank, punched in the number on my ATM card, and was assured that my check would not bounce. I then signed some forms, and the 4runner was mine. I don't remember the length of the entire purchasing process, but it was a lot longer than the time it took to find the 4Runner I wanted. Now, I had to get my 4Runner home. Normally this would not be a problem for anyone. One does not buy a car if one cannot drive. Unless...they've had a TBI. I fell, pun intended, into that category.

To solve this unusual problem, we left Tom's car on the Toyota lot, and he drove my brand new SUV home, with me in it of course. Talk about frustrating. I had just bought a 32 thousand plus dollar car that I'd wanted for years, yet I could not even drive the damn thing home from the dealership. So, I sat in the passenger seat and played with all buttons. That was a pretty expensive ride home, but I didn't care, I was riding in my new 4Runner.

So I returned home with my new 4Runner and attempted to sleep that night. That turned out to be pretty futile. I got up the next day, and just looked at my 4Runner. I sat in the driver's seat and drooled. I thought of how cool it would be to take it mountain biking, or rock climbing, or snowboarding, or road biking, or camping, or just driving in the mud. Then I got an extremely painful bit of reality: I could not do any of those things. I couldn't even drive the thing! Talk about a kick in the crotch. It did, however, motivate me to get my driver's license.

CHAPTER 34

I had an appointment to take the driving portion of the driver's license test in Napa. I was really reluctant to take the test there. The reasons being: Napa has a lot of one way streets which are confusing to me, there are an unusually high number of idiots in Napa, who drive like idiots, and everything looks pretty much the same to me. So I was between a rock and a hard place or, more accurately, between a dull and confusing place.

I had an appointment to take the drivers test. My mom, or dad, I don't remember which, drove me to the DMV in Napa in my brand new 4Runner to take the driving test. I don't really remember taking the test, I just remember passing. When I passed the drivers test for the first time in high school it was really cool. It was a huge step towards being an independent grown up. However, that paled, I mean paled, in comparison to passing it this time. Now all I had to do, was get out of my parents house. After that...well...I didn't have a clue.

I have just remembered something. The shrink, Dr. Tim Berry, whom I was seeing at the time, decided I needed to get out of the house once in a while and do something constructive. He knew that I had really enjoyed my job at Flora Springs Winery and liked all the people I had worked with and for. So during my session one day, Dr. Berry called Flora Springs Winery and talked with Ken, the winemaker. They decided I could come in once week, for a couple of hours, and help Ken out. I would not be doing any cellar work or any wine making stuff, but Ken said I could do some data input on his

115

computer. I knew Ken and figured he did not really relish doing any kind of work on a computer, and I was willing to do anything, so I readily agreed to do it. There was one minor problem. I could not drive there, it was to far to walk, and I was not going to ride a bike...for obvious reasons. It turned out, I could get a ride to the winery on Friday with my dad, and my mom could pick me up a couple of hours later.

Getting my own place was all I could think about. I did not really think about minor details such as how was I going to pay rent or whether I'd get bored and lonely. Those kinds of questions were unimportant at the time.

I looked in the classified ads of the local paper and I looked on bulletin boards around the valley. I was not having much luck. One number I called was for a place in Angwin. The woman who answered I'm sure is very nice, but she was very "short" with me on the phone. The reason being, I had called on a Saturday, which is the Sabbath for Seventh Day Adventists. She told me it was the Lord's day and I should call some other day. I am not at all religious, but it would seem to me, that helping your fellow man would be a good thing to do on the Lord's day. Granted, she had no idea about my situation, but still.

I called a bunch of other places, and looked at a few, but none were even close to what I wanted and/or needed. I was getting, not only discouraged, but pretty pissed-off. One day, I saw an add in the St. Helena Star for a one bedroom apartment next to the Silverado Trail. It sounded good, and was relatively inexpensive. I had my Mom call and setup an appointment to see the place.

The reason I had my Mom call was because my speech was....uhhh....shall we say, hard to understand. I did not want to owners of the place to think I was drunk at 10:00 A.M. on a Wednesday. I did not think that would be good for business. She talked with the owner on the phone, gave him a very brief summary of my situation, and set up a time for us to view the apartment. I did not have a Drivers License at the time, so my

Mom had to drive me to the place.

We found the place for rent, and went inside. I didn't look at the kitchen, or the windows, or the closets, or the carpet. I went straight for the bathroom. The reason being, I wanted to see if the shower could hold my bar.

I had progressed enough in my recovery to not require a transfer bench in the shower. I did, however, require something to hold on too. The medically approved shower bar cost a million dollars...well...not really, but it was not cheap. My dad figured one of those bars that goes in a pickup truck bed to hold in-place whatever is back there, would work just as well. It did. Plus it would be a hell of a lot cheaper than a "proper" bar. I needed this bar to hold onto in order to get into, or out of, the shower, and to keep from falling over in the shower. One can now see why I ran to the shower, first thing. The shower would work.

Now I could check out the rest of the house. It was not a house really; it was a structure next to a house, which had an upstairs apartment and a downstairs apartment. I was interested in the downstairs apartment. It had a big bathroom with a shower I could get in and out of with no help, except from the metal bar. It a had a nice big bedroom, a small kitchen, a small dining area, and a living area. Most importantly, however, it had no parents, sisters, doctors, or therapists. I filled out an application and crossed my fingers. Not long after that, either the next day or the day after, I received word that the place was mine.

I had my own pad! I was really excited for about three minutes, and then reality hit me. I had no job. I had friends but they all had jobs, kids, wives, or at least girlfriends. I had no hobbies. I could not do any of the activities I had done previous to my accident. I was in constant pain. I would have to cook, clean, do laundry, do dishes, amuse myself, live the life of a bachelor all without much money and no income.

A bachelor's life is not bad except I was utterly sick of it. I was really tired of going out drinking and hoping I would get "lucky." That is fun when you are in college and/or just out of college, but it gets old really fast when you have a career and a little bit of responsibility, neither of which I had, but still... Now, it seemed like I was starting that phase of life all over again. As the reader will discern, I had additional bachelor issues.

CHAPTER 35

Despite all this "back to normal" stuff, I still had to go to physical therapy. I had therapy, in St. Helena, at a physical therapy center run by St. Helena Hospital and Health Center. I therefore had the same therapists, Julie being one of them. Boy was I stoked! I had a nice new 4Runner, my driver's license, some cash in the bank, a cool place to live, and Julie Loucks as a therapist. Life could not be better! I don't remember the exact order, or timeframe, in which all this subsequent shit went down. I just know that it happened and I'll probably never recover from some of it.

At this point, I was still seeing my shrink, Dr. Tim Berry. One fine summer day I had an appointment with him. I was having a bad couple of days, so I was looking forward to talking with someone. The joy of having my own place had worn off. I was extremely bored, I was very lonely, I did not see my situation improving, and I was already getting tired of looking at my walls and sitting alone on my couch. For some reason a thought occurred to me. I knew at the St. Helena Hospital and Health Center there was a mental health unit informally known as "Third South." I knew about it because many years ago my mom had volunteered there. The thought occurred to me that it would not be too bad to go there for a couple of days. I mainly wanted a change of scenery, a different couch to sit on, and different views out the window. Plus, I thought maybe I would meet a cute nurse or something and she would take pity on me and come over to my place some time. So, not only was I bored and lonely, I was totally desperate for some female…anything. Therefore I, being the genius that I am, figured I should go to Third South for a couple of days and see what happened. Maybe there would be a good-looking female therapist, or whatever they have. Or maybe some cute patient. Like I said, I was desperate. Problem was, one cannot just go there on one's own and hang-out for a couple of days to see what's shakin'. Since I'm a genius, I knew that a psychologist, for example Tim Berry, would have to give me a referral. During my appointment with Dr. Berry, I asked him about "Third South." I said that maybe I should go there since I was so depressed. I said some things that I figured would get me a me a referral. Now, I'm not real clear on what exactly was said, but I'll give Tim Berry the benefit of the doubt.

I probably, when asked, said that I was not suicidal. I did say, however, when asked, that I was homicidal. I live near the Silverado Trail in the Napa Valley. There are often vacationing people riding bicycles along the Silverado Trail. Often, the riders are not…shall we say…very steady, on their bicycles. In addition, riders with no helmets are quite frequent. This would just piss me off. I would think, *Look at that idiot. Wobbling all over, no helmet, but they'll be fine, they're not a loser like me.*

I told Tim Berry that I felt like running over one of those people, just because I felt like they deserved it. Hopefully, I would not kill them, just permanently screw them up so that they would know what it was like to be me. I then told him I would never actually do it. In reality, I'm a pretty big chicken.

So, Tim Berry called Third South and talked with someone. He then asked me if I wanted him to ask them if they had a bed available. I thought, *Well it certainly can't hurt ask.* So, I said, "Sure." That was the wrong answer.

All this took quite a bit of time. During that time I remembered that the San Francisco Giants were playing the Los Angeles Dodgers, and the game was on TV. The game was going to start in a couple of hours and I wanted to be home to watch it. I love baseball. I can't hit the ball, but I love to watch it. Anyway, getting home to watch the baseball game was my number one priority. So, I told Dr. Berry I did not want anything to do with Third South. I did not want to go there. I did not think that would be any sort of problem. Well...I was wrong.

I do not remember why, maybe I could not drive at this point, but my Mom was picking me up and it was near dinnertime. Dr. Berry spoke with my Mom when she arrived to get me. I don't know what they said, but I'm sure homicide, suicide and Third South were mentioned. My Mom and I then went to dinner, we told Dr. Berry where we were going. I was pretty stoked at this point. I was getting a good dinner, and was then going back to my own place to watch the baseball game. That is when the shit the fan.

Dr. Berry came into the restaurant and asked my mother to come back to his office. She did. I thought it would be a few minutes, but I ended up eating dinner alone in the restaurant. When I was just about done my mother returned to eat her cold food. Pretty quick, Dr. Berry showed up again, and asked me to come back to his office. I said, "O.K.", and followed him back to his office. On the way, I looked at my watch and saw that the baseball game would start in about an hour, so I hoped whatever I was going to Dr. Berry's office for would not take long.

Dr. Berry said he had spoken with my mother, and then he had called his colleague up at Third South. It was told to me that I was going up to Third South to talk with Dr. Berry's colleague, who was an expert on depression. I was not happy about it because I figured I would miss the first pitch of the baseball game, but I figured since I had brought up the whole Third South issue and had mentioned homicide and suicide that I should go. I figured I'd just give all the nice, happy answers, and say that I did not really want to hurt anyone. I figured I would smile a lot, be very agreeable, not say anything threatening to, or about, anyone, and the meeting would be relatively short. Worst case scenario: I would miss the first three or four innings of the baseball game.

Well, I waited for quite awhile in this little cubbyhole type waiting room, getting more upset every second. Finally some guy did show up and I assumed he was Dr. Berry's "colleague." I asked him how long I would have to be there. I was expecting to hear him say something like, "Oh, a half hour or so." Well, I received a bit of a shock. The "colleague" answered, "Oh I don't know, a couple of days." Well, I totally lost it. I just got up and walked out. Of course I could not go very far because the Third South Ward is all locked up, or down. I found a bench to sit on and just fumed. I realized that Dr. Tim Berry, my psychologist, whom I *totally* trusted, had lied to me. I was told by Dr. Berry, that he had arranged for me to talk with an expert on depression. When, in fact, I had been admitted to the mental ward. I was so fucking furious! I was yelling at anyone and everyone. A security guard came and I just cussed him out. I felt *totally* betrayed. That sounds corny but that is how I felt. I could not comprehend how someone with a Ph.D to help people, could do such an awful thing. Plus, and I have no proof of this, but I think my parents were aware of the whole thing. I've never been so mad. Then to top it all off, I was missing the Giants game. I can't really describe how angry I was.

So, I was in the mental ward for two nights and three days. It was, without question, the absolute worst two nights and three days of my life. I'll only share the worst experience I had during my captivity. The first night, I shared a room with this guy who thought he was being watched and followed, so I guess he was paranoid. In the mental ward, there are certain times and one area patients are allowed to smoke. One cannot have cigarettes or matches or a lighter in their possession. I guess this guy smuggled a cigarette out of the smoking area. Problem was he did not smuggle anything to light his cigarette with. That is a problem when one really needs a nicotine fix. Desperate times call for desperate measures. This must have been a desperate time because he came up with a desperate solution.

I was lying in my bed, relaxed, trying to sleep, attempting to survive this ordeal, when I heard a loud "pop" and saw a flash of light. I kept hearing "pops" and seeing flashes of light. I could not figure out what was going on. I rolled on my side and looked at the flashes and where the sound was coming from. As my eyes adjusted to the light, I figured out what was going on, and....I did not like it. My roommate was trying to light his cigarette by, I'm not kidding, sticking a piece of his toothpaste tube into the electrical outlet on the wall, thus creating a spark, and thereby lighting his cigarette. I thought, *Holy shit! If he starts a fire I'm screwed!* Since my brain injury, I have not been able to move fast in any way, shape, or form. I could not run from the room. I just simply can't run. I have a hard enough time just walking. I could not have climbed up, out the window, and down because my right shoulder does not work very well and I have very poor balance. I did not want to tell him to stop because…well…it was a mental ward and I had no idea what he would do. So, needless to say, I did not get a good nights sleep. As far as I know, he didn't get his nicotine fix either. I will give him credit for coming up with a pretty clever way of at least potentially lighting his cigarette. I'm assuming the hospital staff became aware of his shenanigans because, for my next night, I had my own room.

I've tried to forget the rest of my little vacation. I remember I spent a lot of time thinking Dr. Tim Berry was a total fucking joke and that this was all his fault. There is something else I could not get out of my injured brain. The lyrics to the song "Welcome Home (Sanitarium)," by Metallica. Before I go any further, I will tell the reader that before the St. Helena Hospital and Health Center was the St. Helena Hospital and Health Center, it was an actual sanitarium. I was born there, no laughs. Okay, here are the lyrics that kept running through my head:

"Welcome to where time stands still
No one leaves and no one will

Moon is full, never seem to change
Just labeled mentally deranged
Dream the same thing every night
I see our freedom in my sight
No locked doors, no windows barred
No things to make my brain seem scarred.
Sleep my friend and you will see
That dream is my reality
They keep me locked up in this cage
Can't they see it's why my brain says rage
Sanitarium, leave me be
Sanitarium, just leave me alone
Build my fear of what's out there
And cannot breathe the open air
Whisper things into my brain
Assuring me that I'm insane
But violent use brings violent plans
Keep him tied, it makes him well
He's getting better, can't you tell?
No more can they keep us in
Listen, Damn it, we will win.
They see it, they see it well
They think this saves us from our hell
Sanitarium, leave me be
Sanitarium, just leave me alone
Sanitarium, just leave me alone
Fear of living on
Natives getting restless now
Mutiny in the air
Got some death to do
Mirror stares back hard
Kill, it's such a friendly word
Seems the only way
For reaching out again.

The day I was to be released they would not let me go until

I spoke with a certain doctor. My parents and I kept waiting for him, but he did not show up. I was getting really nervous. Finally, I was just allowed to leave. I never saw the doctor I was waiting for. I hope the reader can get a sense of how miserable those couple of days were.

That was not the end of Dr. Timothy Berry. I had another session with him, previously scheduled, I must add. I was not looking forward to it. As one might surmise, I was not very intent on speaking with, or even being in the same room as, Dr. Timothy Berry. I did not, *could* not, trust him.

When I entered his office for my appointment, I could not even look at him. I did, however, put on a happy face and answered all his questions, in a positive, yet totally false, light. I was afraid that if I said anything that was not happy, rosy, loving, or jovial, he would call his "colleague" and I would be in Third South again. I pretended everything was wonderful and said that my stay in the mental ward did me a world of good. It was all feel-good bullshit, of course.

There is a song by the band Pantera that explains absolutely perfectly how I feel about Dr. Timothy Berry. The song is called "War Nerve" and the absolute perfect lyrics are: "All the money in the fucking world couldn't buy me one second of trust or one ounce of faith in anything you're about." That hits the nail on the head. Boy was that episode traumatic. My head trauma from my bicycle crash pales in comparison to what Tim Berry did to my mind. Unfortunately, as the reader will see, that feeling of distrust towards Tim Berry was expanded, by Julie Loucks and Linden Reeves, to include the entire human race.

CHAPTER 36

I'll devote a chapter to the hell that my physical therapy assistant, Julie Loucks, and to a much lesser extent, her boss, Linden Reeves, put me through. Unfortunately, I'm still going through my Julie Loucks hell, probably always will be. This was a worse trauma than a TBI. To this day, I have not even begun to cope with it. If I sound sour, that is because I am very sour, and probably a little immature too. Oh well...I was still a TBI teenager, and as we all know, teenagers are "common sense challenged" due, in part, to raging hormones. Anyway...here goes.

Since I had gotten out of the hospital, and even before I was released, I heard countless times from people how good God must be to have saved my life, how wonderful He, or She, must be to have spared me and there must be some reason, some higher purpose that I did not know of...yet. Well, I thought they were all nuts and just nodded my head and smiled.

Then I went to the St. Helena Hospital and Health Center for physical therapy, occupational therapy, and speech therapy. As mentioned before, that is when, and where, I saw Julie Loucks for the first time. Holy Cow! I was in love...but that damn ring!

To my pleasant surprise, I would often overhear Julie talking with her colleagues and she very often mentioned her boyfriend. Also, I would quite regularly catch her looking at me and she would smile in a very...ahh..."you turn me on" type of way when she noticed me looking at her. I would think, *Dude. Relax. You're totally fucked-up.* I really was. I was in a wheelchair. I could not talk to well. I was wearing my glasses. I was living at home with my parents. I did not feel very "desirable." Yet, here was this incredibly sexy, gorgeous, blonde, with an incredible body, looking at me seductively, and smiling.

As my therapy went on, I realized Julie was not only incredibly sexy, but she actually seemed like she had the type of personality that I had been looking for. I still kept overhearing her mention her boyfriend and she was still wearing that damn wedding ring. Finally, I just got tired of thinking about it, and I asked her about the ring. She said she was not married and the ring was her grandmothers. I then asked her why she wore it on her ring finger, because that meant she was married. The answer I got was not at all what I expected, and I am sure, now, that it was total bullshit. She said she did not realize that a ring on that particular finger meant she was married and she wore the ring because she liked it. I thought, *Hmmm. I thought all women knew what a ring on the ring finger meant. It's in their DNA or something. Oh well, at least she is not married.*

The next time I was at the hospital for therapy, Julie was not wearing the ring. I thought, *Hmmm. What do you know about that?* The more I thought about it the more I liked it. Also, Julie said I had to tell her a joke every time I came for therapy, which was fine with me. She would laugh at every joke I told, which I thought was a great sign. What I did not keep in mind, however, was that I was only a teenager at this point in my TBI years and, as we all know, teenagers do not think rationally on occasion.

Here is what I thought: *My accident did happen for a reason. There must be a God, and I crashed so I would meet Julie, and she would meet me. I've been living lie and there really is a God.* I actually looked forward to going to therapy. I was extremely motivated to get out of my wheelchair. I was bound and determined to get my contacts in and lose my glasses, and I worked extra hard at my speech therapy so I could talk better.

Now skip ahead to me living in my own place. I still had physical therapy but it was in St. Helena at the St. Helena Physical Therapy Center building. This was essentially the physical therapy center from the S.H.H.H.C, but relocated to its own building in St. Helena. It was all the same therapists, including Julie Loucks.

I went to therapy there for a few months. I saw Julie every time I was there so I was happy. What made me even happier was some things she said, and did. She told me I had nice muscles. *That is interesting*, I thought. She told me I had nice, blue eyes. *That is even more interesting*, I thought. One day I was having therapy on my shoulder. I was lying down on my back and Julie was holding my hand and raising it so that my arm was straight. I was then told to move my hand down towards my feet and then up towards my head. I am not really sure of all the details, but after a few minutes of trying to do this, I began to notice something: my fingers had become entwined with Julie's fingers and she was doing all the work, i.e. she was moving my hand down towards my feet and then up towards my shoulder. I know she was doing the work because I had quite doing anything except relaxing and letting her do all the work. Mentally, I was roughly sixteen years old, I had lost most, if not all, of my social knowledge, I was desperate for female attention, in any form, and I was quit lonely. I did not really know what to do, so I didn't do anything.

Not long after that, the insurance company said, "No more therapy on us." On my last day of therapy, I asked Julie for her phone number, thinking she would gladly give it to me. The answer I got was one that, if I had remembered, is the kiss of death for a guy. She said, "Don't call me, I'll call you." However, I didn't remember and as it turned out, the kiss of death would have been a welcome improvement.

So, that was it for physical therapy. At this point, I actually had a job. It had nothing to do with wine or anything that was even remotely close to requiring a college degree, or even a high school diploma. It was in the local movie rental store. The store was about one mile from the physical therapy center where I was having therapy. I stopped at the physical therapy center, soon after I had started working, to let them know I had gotten a job (I had an ulterior motive: to see Julie.) I told them I had a job and told Julie to stop by and say, "Hi," since it was so close to where she worked. She said she would and, of course, I believed her. I was really excited. I thought, *Wow. I can't wait until she stops by. I'll ask her out to dinner or something.* Well, she never stopped by, and since I was a clueless TBI teenager at that point, I did not think anything of it. Plus, I thought we were meant to be together because I heard so often that my accident happened for a reason. I had convinced myself that meeting Julie was the reason.

One day I was returning from a coffee shop in St. Helena, the traffic was really bad, it was hot, I was bored, and I was feeling pretty lonely. The traffic came to a complete stop and I was right next to the entrance to St. Helena Physical Therapy Center. *I thought, Awesome. I'll just pop in there and say "Hi" to Julie.* It was just about their closing time, so I hoped she would not be with a patient. She wasn't. She pretended she was mad at me for not stopping by sooner to visit everyone. She asked why I had not stopped by sooner to visit. I thought, *I have no business being here. Why would I stop?* That is the honest to God truth. It will be evident shortly why that is important. She then said I should stop by more often and visit. I'll repeat that: she said I should stop by more often and visit. I then sat down by her desk while she put away some paper work. She was talking, out loud, with one of her colleagues and I overheard her say something I will never forget. She said that the first thing she did when she got to work was to look and see who was coming in that day. If she saw my name one the list she, knew, "it will be a good day no matter what happens, because he's is coming. He is so funny." I heard that and I just about passed out. I thought, *No way. It can't be.*

I left the P.T. center feeling pretty darn good about life in general. I went back to my place in a good mood. The next day at work, I told the girl I as working with what Julie had said. My co-worker said, "Dude, she likes you." Well, I did not know what the hell I should do now. Remember, I'm a pretty immature teenager at this point. I thought, *Gee, something good is going to come from all shit*! So, I decided to tell her how I felt about her.

I wrote her a letter telling her that I was really attracted to her, that I loved the way she laughed, and I just liked seeing her. I told when and where I worked and that I would like for her to come visit me. I wrote my phone number and e-mail address and said she should call or e-mail me. I was 110% sure she would do at least one of those. Well, she did not do any. I am a very stubborn guy. So I wrote her another letter. I basically complemented her and said I'd like to get to know her better. I did not mail either of these letters. I hand delivered them to the receptionist at the physical therapy place. These letters were probably not the right thing to do, but I had to do something, and that is all I could think of. At the time, I was convinced Julie would welcome the letters and would get in touch me.

Here is how convinced I was: I would vacuum my abode every night, I would do the dishes, clean up the clothes, and tidy up the bathroom a little, because I was positive she would want to see where I lived and I wanted my abode to be female friendly when she came by. I know I seem pathetic and clueless, but I was positive Julie had the hots for me, and I was totally desperate for female...anything. In addition, I was in constant pain, I was very depressed, I was lonely, I was horny, I was mad at the world, and Julie just seemed like a light at the end of the tunnel.

The days went by and I heard nothing from Julie. I could not believe it, I really thought she would contact me. However,

I figured the "ball was in her court" and there was nothing I could do. That is the only sensible decision I made concerning Julie. One day, when I was not working, I went for a bicycle ride. Yes, I still rode my bicycle. Everything went wrong on this bike ride. My feet/shoes kept coming unclipped from the pedals. The chain fell off a couple of times, and my tight, lycra cycling shorts kept getting caught on the front of the seat. It took nearly an hour to ride about two or three miles. I was getting seriously pissed. In St. Helena right near the Pope Street Bridge, there is a little park. There is grass, a table, I think a garbage can, and maybe a bench. Whatever is, or isn't there, it's relatively quiet and peaceful and is relaxing to sit on the grass under a tree. I rode by near the park and decided I would stop there, drink some water, and just relax, because things were not going well.

I sat on the grass, listened to the birds, and tried to figure out my next move. I still wanted to ride my bicycle, but I wanted to avoid streets with much traffic, I especially did not want to ride on, or even cross, Highway 29. There is a lot of traffic on Highway 29.

I got on my bicycle, which was no small accomplishment, and just started riding towards town. I was headed towards Merryvale Winery. I had worked a harvest there a few years before and had become good friends with Bob, the assistant winemaker. I figured I'd pop in and say, "Hello." It was not until I was within fifty yards of the winery that I remembered Bob did not work there anymore. I thought, *Oh, great. Now what?* As I was riding up to Merryvale Winery, it dawned on me that the St. Helena Physical Therapy Center was right next to Merryvale. I was not planning on stopping at St. Helena Physical Therapy. However, I did need to use the parking lot in order to turn around without getting off my bicycle. As I was going through the parking lot, I saw Julie and another male therapist walking through the parking lot, back to work. I thought, *Holy cow! There is a God.* The reason I thought that was because all the "malfunctions" of bicycle equipment I had dealt with delayed me the exact amount of time required for me to bump into Julie in the parking lot. Also because I happened to forget that Bob did not work at Merryvale any longer. I thought, *What are the chances of me bumping into Julie? There is something else at work here.*

I stopped and talked with Julie and the therapist she was with. As she was leaving to go back to work, I asked if she had received the two letters I had written. She said she had. I then asked her if she had read the letters, she said she had and that, "...they were good. I'll call you." Well, I did not think that my life could get much better, and I was right, it couldn't, and wouldn't. I rode my bike back to my humble abode and was actually feeling good about being alive.

I was looking forward to getting up the next morning, because I thought I was going to get a chance to talk with Julie, and she could see what a great guy I was. That lasted about three or four days, and then I realized she was not going to call. I should have just said, "Oh well," but, of course, I didn't.

Previously, Julie had said I should stop by and visit, so I did. Once I was on a bicycle ride and stopped by just to see what was going on. On another occasion, traffic was really bad, so I stopped to let the traffic thin out. Both times I was told Julie was very busy and that I should come back another day. That was fine by me. Then one day was I really down about my whole situation and I really wanted to just see Julie. I stopped by physical therapy during business hours hoping I would get lucky and Julie would be free. I really don't know if she was free or not. I waited a few minutes and then Julie walked out into the hallway talking on her cell phone. I heard bits and pieces of her end of the conversation and it very clearly was a personal phone call. I heard the "Goodbye's" and Julie returned to the physical therapy room. I got all excited because I figured Julie would be out momentarily. I figured wrong. After a while of waiting, the receptionist told me that Julie was really busy and I should, "Come back some other day." I was *never* told not to come back. If I had been, I would not have come back.

I just remembered what prompted me to write those letters to Julie. After my therapy had ended I had not seen Julie, or any of my therapist, for quite some time. One morning I was driving to a local coffee shop and was stopped at a red light. A really attractive blonde, with a very...shall I say "hot" body, jogged in front of me. The jogger looked at me, smiled, and waved. I was dumbfounded. I thought *Does she know me? Do I know her? How could I forget a babe like that? She must think I'm someone else, because no girl that gorgeous knows me.* I kept thinking that my TBI had caused me to forget about some cute blonde that had known. The light turned green and I went on my way. However, I could not shake the feeling that I knew that jogger. Then it hit me. *That was Julie!* Then I thought, *No, it couldn't be. Julie is not that busty.* However, I could not shake the feeling that it was Julie I had seen. I was sure it was her. But I knew it couldn't be Julie because the jogger's boobs were too big. Unless...One day I could not take it anymore, so I stopped at the physical therapy place, at the end of the day, and asked Julie if she had been "enhanced." She said, "Yes."

Shortly thereafter, she said something that she had said quite often before, but I have forgotten to mention it. She said, "I'm still not married. I don't think I'll ever get married." I almost proposed to her right then and there. I had not asked her if she was married. I did not hint that I was thinking about that. Yet, she just came right out and said it. I thought, *Hmmm, that's interesting. Why would she tell me that...again?*

I did not know what the hell was going on. I thought my injured brain was confused and playing tricks on me. *Did this chic like me? Was I just so desperate I was just imagining what she was saying?* I was *totally* confused. Plus, I was looking for something, anything, good to come out of this pure hell I was going through.

In summary: I had written those two letters, I had stopped by the physical therapy place where she worked, I had even stopped by and left her a note, asking her to call me. All this time I thought she did not mind me trying to get in touch with her. I was never told anything by her, or her coworkers, that I was doing anything unwanted. Of course, I did not quite understand the whole "silent treatment" implications. The reader must understand that I'm basically a horny teenager, so I do not think like a rational human being. I kept hoping she would call for a week or so, then I just got mad. I wrote her another letter. However, this was not a "nice" letter.

I called her some ah...umm...not publicly visible body parts. I degraded her boyfriend and told her what I thought of her totally ignoring me. I did not, repeat not, threaten her in any way, shape, or form. I sent the letter to St. Helena Physical Therapy Center and hoped it would ruin her day. I do not know if it did or not, but she certainly decided I was useless, and got the last laugh.

Every day that I work at the video store, I take a break at 11:30 A.M. and walk to the corner gas station and get a cup of coffee. On this day, which was a few days after I mailed the not so "nice" letter to Julie, I returned from the gas station to find two police officers waiting for me in the video store. They said I was not in any trouble that they just wanted to talk to me. The key words are "talk to," not "talk with." They did not let me get a word in edge wise. I was attempting to tell them what Julie had said to me time and time again. I don't really know why I was trying to tell them that, but I had to do something. The cops said that Julie had shown the "nice" letter to a friend, and the friend told her to call the police, which she did, obviously. The cops told me not write Julie anymore letters, not to go to where she worked, not to see her, just leave her alone. Then they left. Fortunately, the boss was not there.

I could not contemplate what was going on. I was in shock. My whole world was shaken and stirred. I was truly dumbfounded. I could not believe what the cops were saying. I kept thinking, *Did I miss something? I must be really fucking stupid to miss that. Am I that ugly? I must be a repulsive freak for a girl to call the cops on me. What the fuck is wrong with me? How could I miss this? Am I forgetting something?*

I was bewildered. I was totally convinced that Julie had the hots for me, but the cops standing in front of me dispelled that myth in a hurry. The cops just kept telling me to leave Julie alone, how she did not want anything to do with me. It does not stop there, however. A couple of days later I received a letter in the mail from the St. Helena Hospital and Health Center. I'll let the reader read the letter because I really have nothing to say.

Dear Mr. Gosling,

I am Julie Loucks' Supervisor and am writing this letter on her behalf. Recently Julie Loucks informed me that you have been attempting to communicate with her personally and by letter. This has been unwanted communication. She demands that it stop and as her Supervisor I am directing you not to communicate with her in any way.

You have been a patient in Physical Therapy several times over the past several years. I understand that you have benefited from the treatments that you received and have gotten to know the staff very well. At present you are not a patient in St. Helena Physical Therapy and have no cause to be on the Physical Therapy premises.

Thank you in advance for your cooperation in this important matter.

Linden Reeves PT
Rehab Services Team Leader

When I received this letter, I just shook my head and sat down on my couch. I was speechless. I thought, *Why does she hate me so much? Am I that much of a freak? Why does she lie to me? I do what she says I should do, and then she does this?* I could not stop asking, *Why does she lie to me?* I said to myself, *She said I should stop by and visit, so I do, and then, not only are the police called, but I get this letter from her boss.* I kept thinking, *Why does she lie to me all the time? No one is that lame.* Well, I've been wrong before. That was it. My brain, what was left of it anyway, just said, "O.K. I've had it. No more. This is bullshit!"

I have thought for days, for months...no for years, about what to say now. I can't describe it. I will, for the readers benefit, give it a shot. I did not feel like a person. My ego was absolutely destroyed. My self-esteem was totally destroyed. My self-image was, at best, completely shattered. I was shocked. When I was in the hospital and told I had been in a bicycle crash, I honestly was not to surprised, but this was just out of the blue, at least that is what I thought. I often hear about a child's self-esteem in school, and how it should not be hurt, or diminished, or anything like that. I used to just scoff at that and think, *What a bunch of wussies these kids are these days.* Well, my opinion on that subject changed.

It shouldn't take a great leap of thought or imagination to realize I did not get much sleep that night, or the next, or the next, or...I could not figure out what was wrong with me but I figured it had to be something major because one does not call the police *and* one's boss just because their friend, whom you've never even seen, says you should. I could not turn my thoughts off at night. I just kept thinking, *What the hell is wrong with me?* Plus, my whole comfort, or solace, or something, I had taken in thinking that this crash had actually happened for a reason, was shot to hell. I just kept thinking, *I ruined my life for no fucking reason at all.* Now, the depression came.

I had to do...something...anything. So I wrote a letter to Linden Reeves. I explained the situation to him, told him what had been said to me, by Julie and the other people working there. My mom hand delivered the letter to him. Shortly thereafter I received an e-mail from him that said he had received my letter, would take it into consideration, and "keep it on file." That was the most chickenshit response that I could think of. Even to this very day, I can't think of anything less chickenshit. I could not believe it. My depression came faster and harder now.

Depression leads to...a lot of bad shit. I could not sleep and lack of sleep leads to more shit. I had boatloads of shit. I only worked three hours a day, so I had way too much time to think about all of the shit I had. My existence would not have been so bad if I could have gotten some sleep. I would not even get into bed until two or three A.M., and then all I would do was just stare at the dark ceiling. I must have dozed off a little because I am still alive, but I did not get out of bed feeling rested. I was constantly tired, and as a result, I always in a pissy mood. The first thing I would do in the morning was to figure when I could get back in bed and at least try and sleep.

CHAPTER 37

In the _Oxford American Dictionary_ the word "trauma" is defined as: "emotional shock producing a lasting effect upon a person." The word "traumatic" is defined as "of or causing trauma." I would have to say that this whole Julie/Linden episode was the very definition of traumatic. In fact, it trumped every other trauma I have endured. It was my "trump trauma" if you will. My hitting a pick-up truck at 50 MPH on a bicycle, my being lied to by a "professional" psychologist, my captivity in a mental ward for three days, was just a little scratch compared to the emotional, mental...anything and everything trauma I went through with Julie Loucks and Linden Reeves. Believe it or not, things keep going downhill from here. My gums still hurt.

Psychologists really do help, if you get a good one. I needed to see one because of my depression and the fact that I could not sleep. Tim Berry was out of the question, for obvious reasons. Dr. Bodor recommended a lady he knew, So I gave her a try. Her name was Dr. Mansen. Strike one. Her husband was Dr. Green from acute rehabilitation at Queen of the Valley Hospital. Strike two. It takes three strikes before you are out, so she had one strike left.

I had a few sessions with her and they were fine. However, she did some work at a mental hospital, or something, and as a result, she was often late. At first it was just a few minutes late, which was acceptable, understandable, no big deal. However, the lateness kept getting longer and longer, to where finally she would just cancel. That just pissed me off. I don't really know why, but I could not deal with driving down to Napa from my place in St. Helena, for an appointment, which had been made days before, only to find out Dr. Mansen, was not there. Strike three, you're out. I was already very anti-psychologist thanks to Tim Berry, and this did nothing to change my opinion. I did not see her again.

Prior to this, Dr. Mansen arranged for me to see a colleague of hers who dealt with depression. He came to my humble abode and talked with me about a program he ran. He gave me a "test" to see how depressed I really was. I answered the questions, and gave the test back to him. He went through my answers, wrote down a number for each of my answers, and then totaled the numbers to get a final score. He then compared the score I had gotten with a table of results to see how depressed I was. Problem was, he did this right in front of me. I was able to, quit easily, figure out the scoring system and the table, and therefore could get whatever score I wanted. Therefore, I could be as depressed or happy as I wanted him to think I was.

I'll quickly explain the test and scoring system. It's really simple. The test consists of about twenty questions or so. Each question had five answers. It was multiple choice. Each answer was assigned a number from 1 to 5. The first answer, #1, was always a cheerful, forgiving, not hostile type of answer. The last answer, #5, was always a depressed, pissed-off, hateful, angry type of answer. Once the patient had answered all the questions, the shrink added up the number of all the answers that had been given. That was the patient's score. The higher the score the more depressed the person was.

My score was quite high, so the shrink said I should take the test again. So I did. This time, however, I knew what my score would mean and how to get that score. So I answered #4 or #5 to all the questions, I did not even read all the questions. I was basically just messing with the guy because he was a psychologist. He "evaluated" my second test, and told me no one had ever gotten that high of a score before (the higher the score, the more depressed you are). Therefore, I was the most depressed person he had come across. I thought, *Well gee, I can score higher if you want.* Unfortunately, I probably should not have done that.

This shrink informed me of a program he was involved for people with mental "issues." We talked about it and he was convinced it would do me some good, seeing how depressed I was. I told him I would enroll in the program if, and only if, my insurance would pay for it. He said he would look into it and let me know the details when he came next week for another session.

I spoke with my parents about the program, and they thought it sounded pretty good. A week passed, the shrink returned for my next session, and told me he had learned what my insurance would pay for. He had determined that the insurance company would cover only two of the three daily sessions in the program. In addition, the insurance would only cover three days a week. I said, "O.K. Let's go for it."

The program was called "Transitions" and was held in Napa. The program would send a taxi to bring me to the program and then, of course, take me home. I thought that was pretty cool since gas was ridiculously expensive. The program was all right, I guess, but I did not benefit from it. In fact, I just became more disgusted with psychologists. Let me explain.

One of the psychologists we were required to speak with was Dr. Thuma. None of the patients liked him. Not because he asked tough questions that made your look at yourself, but because he would ask unprofessional questions that were none of his business. I'll give you an example. When I was talking with him, he asked me where I lived. That was fine, so I told him. Then he asked what I paid for rent. I asked, "What does that matter?", and did not tell him. He then went on to say how St. Helena was very expensive, how he had friends who could not afford to live there, and how he, himself, probably could not afford to live there. I thought, *That's nice. Who cares? You are not helping me with anything.* I do not remember much else of that meeting. I do remember that he acted, and seemed, extremely condescending. He gave the impression that he was too good to have to deal with these fucked-up, lower class people.

Then came the straw that broke the camel's back, as far as Dr. Thuma and Transitions were concerned. I was leaving a grocery store in too-expensive-for-psychologists-to-live St. Helena and I saw this guy riding his bicycle with a kid sitting in a "trailer" type contraption attached behind his bike. There was at least one other kid with them on his own bicycle. The guy turned out to be Dr. Thuma. This does not seem significant in any way until I present the last fact: everyone was wearing a bicycle helmet except Dr. Thuma. Now, I'm no psychologist or parent...but...it seems to me that is not a very good idea. I think the kids are thinking, "This helmet is hot and uncomfortable. I don't want to wear it. Gee, look. When I'm older I won't need to wear one." It also brings in the whole "Do as I say, not as I do," issue. I am guessing that is not the best way to raise children.

At first I was disgusted with the whole scene. Then I just chuckled. Here is a well-educated (supposedly) professional. He is a trained psychologist who should know how people's actions affect the beliefs, actions, thoughts, and emotions of other people. However, here he is committing, what I think is a gross and obvious error. The whole "Do as I say, not as I do," issue, may have serious negative and long-lasting implications to everyone involved in the near, and not so near, future. In addition, should some accident occur, Dr. Thuma is greatly increasing his chances that his kids will be changing his diapers. I lost any, and all respect for Dr. Thuma, not that I had much to begin with. That was the beginning of the end of my "Transitions" involvement.

I went a few more times, but I could not, in any way take it seriously. One day I was alone in one of the rooms with one of the female counselors, who was roughly my age. I do not remember why I did this, what led up to it, or why I was alone in this room with her. I just remember what happened. The counselor upset me somehow, and I just snapped. I cussed her out as brutal and as personal as I could. I used every cuss word I knew (which took some time). I used every female body part, and its function, in my verbal tirade. She just got up and went to her office. I cane to my senses shortly after that and went to apologize. She would not let me into her office so I apologized through the door.

At the next session, I had a meeting with the psychologists, and the counselor I had verbally abused. I apologized, told the counselor that it was nothing personal, that I would have done the same thing to whomever happened to be in the room with me. The psychologists, including Dr. Thuma, gave me a bunch of intelligent sounding drivel as to why I had reacted the way I had and what I could do to resolve the feelings, emotions, and whatever other crap they could think of.. When it was time for me to go home, everyone felt better about the situation.

I started referring to it as "Transitional hell" because going there was just awful. It was a voluntary program, so I could quit whenever I wanted. I wanted to quit, so I did. I told one of the therapists that I did not want to come anymore, and of course, they tried to change my mind. I was on the verge of changing my mind, when I saw Dr. Thuma. He just looked so arrogant and condescending, that I just got pissed-off and made up my mind to quit. The story does not end here, unfortunately.

A couple of weeks passed, and then I got a bill in the mail. The bill was for "Transitions." I don't remember the exact amount, but it was a pretty hefty amount, two or three thousand dollars. I did not understand why I had gotten the bill, since I had only taken the sessions that my insurance would pay for. I have absolutely no proof of this, but I think those damn psychologists were envious of the fact that I was able to live in St. Helena, drove a nice 4Runner, did not kiss the ground they walked on, and was able to think for myself. So they sent me a bill.   I did not pay the bill, but I showed it to my mom and then the bill disappeared. She says she did not take it, but I'm so conditioned to anybody and everybody lying to me, that I don't believe her. I hope she did not pay it. If I sound bitter and jaded that is because I am, especially when it comes to psychologists and the St. Helena Hospital and Health Center. I must mention that Transitions was a program that was under, or run by, or financed by, or founded by, or all of the above, the St. Helena Hospital and Health Center. Believe it or not, I had one more experience with the St. Helena Hospital and Health Center that was not good, but it's for later. I still could not sleep, and it was becoming a problem.

CHAPTER 38

When I was in college, I saw a bumper sticker that said, "...I'll sleep when I'm dead." At the time, I thought that was one of the dumbest things I had ever seen. I figured it belonged to some pseudo stud that was trying to make people, especially women, think he was a "cool, studly, dude." Now, it would just absolutely piss me off when I thought about it because I figured the guy who owned it was probably an asshole, probably had a girlfriend or at least dated women, and certainly had never had some chic call the cops on him. I would think about that, amongst other things, at night when I could not sleep. I imagine that the great majority of heterosexual, single, twenty-five to thirty year old males, think predominately about women, at night. I could not conceive of a women calling the cops on me. I lost every single molecule of self-confidence and self-esteem. I began to think I must be a repulsively ugly freak of some sort. If not that, had I said something awful? Had I done something threatening? I thought I must be an absolute total fucking loser for a girl to call the cops on me and I got even more depressed. Nights were a living hell. I would be so tired and depressed in the morning, I had to psyche myself up just to get out of bed. I forced myself to eat breakfast, because I was not hungry and I did not really give a shit if I lived or died. I was still in shock that Julie had called the cops as a first option. I could understand the police being called if she had told me to leave her alone or if she had gotten a friend or a co-worker to tell me to leave her alone, and I didn't. But calling the police as a first resort was just...unthinkable. I thought, *God damnit! What the hell is wrong with me? Am I that gross?* This was all before I got dressed. My gums still hurt.

I was full of self-doubt. I thought I was misunderstanding anything, and everything, anybody said to me. I lost absolutely every shred of self-confidence. I couldn't take it. As a result I could not sleep. Therefore, I was extremely tired all of the time. That led to the negative thoughts, which led to self-hateful thoughts, which led to depression, which led to no sleep, which led to.... This was, or is, the definition of a "vicious cycle." It was becoming a problem. I had to break the cycle.

Before I go any further, I would like to share with the reader the lyrics of a song that is just perfect. The song expressed exactly how I felt about all the shit that had been said and done to me by Julie Loucks, Dr. Tim Berry, and the shrinks at Transitions. The song is called "River of Deceit" and is by Mad Season.

My pain is self-chosen
At least, so The Prophet says
I could either burn
Or cut off my pride, and buy some time
A head full of lies is the weight, tied to my waist

The River of Deceit pulls down
The only direction of flow is down
Down, oh down
Down, oh down
Down, oh down
Down, oh down

My pain is self-chosen
At least I believe it to be
I could either drown
Or pull off my skin and swim to shore
Now I can grow a beautiful shell for all to see

CHAPTER 39

St. Helena Hospital and Health Center, I get shivers just typing the name, has a sleep clinic. So, I went there (that's how desperate I was). They put me in a room and hooked me up to a bunch of electrodes. Then I was left alone to sleep. However, it was still light outside, I was not at all tired, plus I hated being in that hospital. As part of the sleep treatment, I was to be awakened at regular intervals throughout the night, at least that is what I was told. Does anyone see a problem here? If one cannot sleep, how can one be awakened? So I spent a sleepless night in S.H.H.H.C., just getting more and more upset every time someone came in to awaken me. I left the next day as the "treatment" was concluded. My gums still hurt.

The electrodes to which I had been hooked to all "night" recorded all kinds of brain waves, heart rate, and lots of other stuff that I have no clue about. I put "night" in quotes because I had no idea what time it was when the treatment started, except that it was still light outside, or what time it was when the treatment was finished. Anyway, a doctor had to evaluate all the data that had been collected during my "sleep." I assumed the results of my night with the electrodes would give the doctor some hint as to why I could not fall asleep, and how to resolve the problem. Well, one should never assume. I went back to S.H.H.H.C. to meet with the doctor who had evaluated all the data. I was looking forward to going back because I was really tired and needed a good nights sleep. I met the doctor and sat in his office while he flipped through page after page of data. He did this for quite some time, asked me a few questions, and then resumed flipping pages of data. The doctor then quit flipping through the data, sat back in his chair, looked at me and said, "Well, you can't sleep. Why do you think that is?" I said, "Isn't that what your are supposed to tell me?" I do not remember anything else of that meeting because I was too busy trying to figure out how I had gotten to the fourth dimension. Well, not really, but one must admit that one would expect a better response than the one I received. As I left the meeting, the doctor extended his hand for me to shake but I did not take it. I don't shake hands with people I have absolutely no respect for.

I still could not sleep. There is a sleep clinic in Palo Alto that is run by Stanford University. I went there. I don't remember much about it, except that I was hooked to electrodes and told to try and sleep. It was during the night time, at least. They came up with results that tried to explain my not being able to sleep, which I thought was the point of the whole shebang. The Stanford sleep clinic figured that I could not sleep because my brain would just not shut down. It always going a 100 miles an hour, so to speak. This, I figured, was the correct diagnosis.

Despite all this medical and psychological mumbo jumbo, I knew why I could not sleep The main reason was because I had been so mentally traumatized by Julie Loucks calling the cops on me. I was so shocked that a person would actually do that, I could not take it. Additional reasons were: the letter I received from Linden Reeves, the shit that Transitions and those shrinks had pulled, and last but certainly not least, Tim Berry's little lie. It was all too much for my injured, happy-go-lucky brain to deal with. I could not stop my brain from being furious with these people and from thinking what a repulsively ugly guy I must be. I can't put into words how awful those people made me feel about myself. Loser. Worthless. Repulsive. Useless. Ugly. Disgusting. Gross. Freak. Elephant man. These were/are the closest words, or descriptions, I could come up with, but they are not really that close. As the reader might guess, I was not a happy camper. I was not even an unhappy camper, either. I was a totally depressed, pissed-off, disgusted, paranoid, suicidal, homicidal…omnicidal camper. At least I was some sort of camper. I certainly could not be an actual camper.

I still could not sleep, however. Something had to be done. I tried listening to music at night. Don't worry; I did not listen to Metallica, Pantera, or anything like that, although those bands would not have hurt anything. I did listen to Enya, as I had in the hospital. This improved my sleep, or lack of, a small amount. My brain still would not stop hating the afore mentioned "people." I could not stop my brain from thinking what a loser I was, how I had ruined my life, and how I had no hope of ever getting married or having kids because I was so repulsively ugly. I dreaded going to bed.

I cannot adequately express how Julie, Linden Reeves, and my shrinks made me feel about myself. The best description I have come across is from the band Megadeth in their song entitled "A Tout Le Monde":

Don't remember where I was
I realized life was a game
The more seriously I took things
The harder the rules became
I had no idea what it'd cost
My life passed before my eyes
I found out how little I accomplished
All my plans denied

So as you read this know my friends
I'd love to stay with you all
Please smile when you think of me
My body's gone that's all

A tout le monde
A tout les amis
Je vous aime

Je dois partir
These are the last words
I'll ever speak
And they'll set me free

If my heart was still alive
I know it would surely break
And my memories left with you
There's nothing more to say

Moving on is a simple thing
What it leaves behind is hard
You know the sleeping feel no more pain
And the living are scarred

I would lie on my bed and listen to that song over and over again, overdosing on hate, anger, and depression.

At this time, I was also seeing a general physician, Dr. Hynote, who specializes in nutrition. She had me try a boatload of different sleeping pills. Not all at once, mind you. None of them worked. I also tried eating certain foods, all to no avail. I was still just totally mentally and emotionally screwed up, not to mention my gums still hurt like hell. I could not sleep. It was starting to get on my nerves.

One remedy that the Stanford doctors suggested was simply contact with other people. Sounds simple. However, my friends had careers, or wives, or kids, or new homes, or some combination of these and were very busy with their own lives. I could not really just "hang out" with them. I couldn't meet people doing the things I enjoyed: mountain biking, rock climbing, or working in winery, because I could not do those things. It's pretty hard to be sociable when you are sitting on your couch watching TV or playing video games. Plus, thanks to Julie and those fuckin' shrinks, I did not trust anybody, I was paranoid of people, and I just plain did not like people.

My Mom suggested I volunteer somewhere. *Okay,* I

thought, *but where?* A recently healthy, active, young, single, college graduate does not think to much about volunteering, unless, of course, it is volunteering to catch cheerleaders working on their jumps. My Mom then suggested I volunteer at We Care, the local animal shelter. That did not sound too bad because the only thing animals really care about is that you feed them and don't hurt them. Plus, they can't talk to you, so therefore, they cannot lie to you. That was a huge point in their favor. So I volunteered there. All I did was play with the kittens. All the kittens were in a little room with nothing to do, so I would shake a string, or throw little toy critters for them to chase, or roll a ping-pong ball for them to play with. I could not go outside to throw a ball or play with the dogs because I could not throw very well, I could fall easily, and I would get really tired. I volunteered there until I got my job at the local video store. I still could not sleep.

My mother also suggested I volunteer at the Veteran's Home in Yountville. I said I would if she found out all about it and made all the necessary phone calls. She did, and so I started volunteering at the Veterans Home. As of this writing, I still volunteer there once a week. I like going there. Those old guys bust me up. I still could not sleep and my gums still hurt.

I do not know how, why, or when I figured this out, but it turned out that audio books would just knock me out. Not any book, just books read by men. If it were a woman reading the book, I would just get depressed and pissed-off, probably because of what Julie had done to me. It turned out that Western Novels worked really well. Ones written by Louis L'Amour or Max Brand worked the best. The books written by Max Brand and read by Barry Corbin worked magic. I know the first few chapters of those westerns by heart, but I don't know how they end, because I always fall asleep. I have a good idea how they end because they are all pretty much the same. The main character clears his name, gets the bad guys, and ends up with the girl. It never fails and they are so cheesy. I love 'em.

Now that I could actually sleep and get some rest, I actually felt like doing stuff. One thing I still loved doing was riding a bicycle. I had decided by now that the road bicycle may not be the best activity for me. However, I did not make the extremely logical bit of reasoning that riding a mountain bike might not be a good activity for me either. No one ever accused me of being a genius. Anyway, one fine day, I decided I should ride my mountain bike up near my parent's house where I had ridden hundreds of times before. I found a new dirt road, which I had not ridden on previously. So, of course, I rode on it. The road was a few feet wide, covered with small stones, and went down, not sharply, but steadily. I was cruising down the dirt road, thinking what a repulsively ugly, loser I must be and not really paying attention. I decided I was going way too fast. To remedy this, I decided to slow down. Well, easier said than done. I am not really sure what I did, or did not do, but I crashed...hard. I was on the ground in major pain and I could not breath. I have knocked the wind out of myself before but this was a whole new level. I was truly scared because I simply could not breath, plus my shoulder and side hurt like you know what and my knee was bloody. I figured I was going to die right then and there from lack of oxygen. Obviously, I got my breath back and survived. I tried to get on my bike in order to go back to my car, but I could not get on the bike, it was too painful. However, I did not have much choice, because I was out in the middle of a field with no one around. I'll say right now that I was breaking my own first and most important rule of mountain biking: never, repeat never, go alone. This was a rule just for this exact scenario I was in: I crashed, I was in major pain, I could not get on the bike, I had no way of contacting anyone (I'm totally against cell phones, but that's another story.) So I started walking, which was very painful, with my mountain bike back to my 4Runner. Fortunately, and embarrassingly, I had been riding for only a few minutes and so had not gone too far from where I had started. I returned from whence I came and discovered I had a new challenge: get my damn bike on the bike rack! I managed to get my keys out of my bicycling jersey pocket, which was no small, painless feat. Then, I got my mountain bike halfway on the bike rack, and since it was so painful and my parents lived close by, I figured that was good enough. Then, I very gingerly got into the drivers seat, and drove the five minutes to my parent's house. When I arrived, I just very gingerly got out of my car and said I have to get to the emergency room. My Mom asked, "What happened? Are you O.K.?" I answered, "I crashed. I have to go to the emergency room. I think I broke my shoulder and maybe some ribs." Seriously, I knew what I had probably done because normally when I crash on my mountain bike, I only get scrapes and bruises, and I knew this crash was much worse. My Mom then gave a classic mom response. She said, "Well, let's clean up your knee first." To which I replied, "No! Let the hospital do it! Let's go, NOW!" I was not feeling very chipper at the moment.

I painfully struggled, with some help, into my Mom's car and off we went. Where did we go? Well, none other than the St. Helena Hospital and Health Center emergency room. I went in there, got my knee cleaned up, had X-Rays taken, and found out that I did, in fact, have a broken collarbone and three cracked ribs. Now this all sounds like it was quick, simple, and easy. Well, nothing could be further from the truth. There was a lot of waiting, paper work to fill out, more waiting, and a lot of discomfort. I was lying down, which was good, but it hurt like hell to move even a tiny bit, and I was not comfortable. Someone eventually came and cleaned up my knee, but that was it. I kept being told the doctor would be in shortly and I guess he was if you are on an "existence-of-human-life" time scale. However, I was on a "major pain-getting-really-hungry" time scale so it did not seem like a short wait to me.

Finally, the doctor showed up and I was wheeled to an X-Ray room for X-Ray's, strangely enough. That took awhile, but at least I was doing something. I actually saw the X-Ray of my collarbone and it was pretty nasty looking. It looked like a dry, old stick that had just been broken in two. I saw my rib X-Rays also, but they looked fine to me, I just had to assume the doctor knew what the hell he was looking at. Apparently, when one fracture's ones ribs, there is a possibility of a collapsed or punctured lung. Therefore, I had to spend the night in the St. Helena Hospital and Health Center for observation. So, I was wheeled into a hospital room, and that's when the "fun" began.

My left collarbone had just been snapped in half. My right deltoid muscle did not work properly from my bicycle vs. pick-up truck collision. I was in a lot of pain and I was becoming extremely hungry. I had been given water a couple of times but I had been at the hospital for hours and I was extremely hungry. The nurse brought in some "food" on a tray and put it in front of me. Problem was, both of my shoulders were not functioning so I could not get the "food" from the tray into my mouth. So there sat the "food", looking at me and me looking at it. Fortunately, it was hospital "food" so I was not missing much. I was hungry, however, and I could not eat. That really sucks, even if the "food" does require quotation marks. My brother-in-law was visiting me in the hospital at the time so he was able to put food in my mouth. When I was done eating, my brother-in-law went out to speak with the nurses about how I was unable to feed myself. The nurses told him that they were understaffed and could not spare anyone to come feed me. My brother-in-law returned to my room and told me what the nurse had said. Well, that just pissed me off. Let me explain.

Every year, the Napa Valley has a big wine auction. One of the main beneficiaries is the St. Helena Hospital and Health Center. It receives millions of dollars every year from this fund raiser. Now, this in itself, is totally hypocritical. The SHHHC is run by Seventh Day Adventists who, it turns out, believe alcohol to be bad, or evil, or something like that. Yet, they certainly do not refuse money that comes from the consumption of alcohol. Where does this money go? Beats me, but it certainly does not go to patient care, otherwise they would employ enough workers to give the injured patients proper care. It gets worse.

At night, the hospital has a lot of young volunteers, who I am pretty sure are students from the Seventh Day Adventist college, Pacific Union College (P.U.C.), which is in nearby Angwin. So far, so good. During my first night in the S.H.H.H.C., I had somehow managed to slide down towards the foot of my bed and get all twisted up in the sheets. I was very uncomfortable. I could not really pull myself up and straighten myself, or the sheets, out due to my freshly broken left shoulder, my fractured ribs, and my much less than 100% operational right shoulder (from my original crash). So, I did what I thought I was supposed to do. I pressed the button to call a nurse, which would have been one of the young volunteers. Well, I pressed and pressed the button. I could hear people out in the hall talking and laughing and having a good time, but no one came into my room. I thought the button must not work but I could hear a soft "ding" whenever I pressed the call button. Finally, a young female came in and asked what I needed. I said I was all tangled up at the foot of my bed, and that I needed to be straightened out and pulled up towards the top of the bed. Before I tell the reader her response, let me remind the reader of the situation: I have a broken collarbone. I have three cracked ribs. I could likely have a punctured or collapsed lung. I am in a lot, repeat a lot, of pain. I'm quite hungry and tired. I have slid down in my hospital bed towards the bottom, or foot. My sheets are all tangled up. I'm uncomfortable, and most importantly, I'm in a ***HOSPITAL!*** Without further ado, here is her absolutely classic response: "What do you want me to do about it?" Once I got over my initial shock of her answer, I said, "Well, pull me up, straighten me out, and fix the sheets." She said, "Well, wait a sec. Let me get someone." I thought, *O.K. she is not very big. She probably can't move me around very well*. So I waited, and waited. I could hear young people out in the hall talking and doing a lot of laughing. I could hear doors slamming but no one came into my room. Finally, I got mad and started pressing my call button constantly. Eventually, a young, male volunteer came in and got me straightened out and comfortable. However, I was so fucking pissed-off at this point that there was no way I could relax and go to sleep.

I spent the rest of the night just fuming. I was so furious by the time morning came around that I don't remember much of the rest of my stay. I do remember one thing, however. The doctor who was in charge of me, wanted me to get this apparatus that I was to breath into. This was to make sure that I did not have a collapsed or punctured lung. However, no one brought me the apparatus. I just laid there in bed and watched really lame daytime television. Well, I guess I remember two things. I also remember getting morphine shots for all the pain I was in, which was quite a bit. I loved that stuff. I would get a shot and the pain would just...go away. Once the pain was gone, I felt like getting up and moving around. I was really sick of lying in bed watching Jerry Springer interviewing women who had caught their husbands sleeping with their goldfish or having an affair with their neighbors cat.

I kept waiting for my breathing apparatus, but it never came. I still could not feed myself to well and since the hospital had no money to hire additional nurses and was understaffed, I had to rely on family members to feed me. I was not a happy camper. I ended up spending another night in S.H.H.H.C. partly, if not solely, because I had never received my breathing apparatus. I just kept wondering where all the money the S.H.H.H.C. received from the wine auction had gone. My gums still hurt. The morphine did not do anything for the pain there.

The next day, the doctor got me the breathing apparatus, I checked out okay, and was released. I was so happy to be out of that hell hole, A.K.A. The St. Helena Hospital and Health Center. I would never go back there, so I decided to sell my mountain bike.

I had to be driven everywhere again because it is very hard to drive with a broken collarbone, not to mention three cracked ribs. Before that, however, I had to recover for a while. So I had to move back in with my parents. Oh boy! I could not wait for that, no offense mom and dad. It was just going to be there for a few days so I was not too concerned. To be honest, it was not going to be all that bad. I would have meals cooked for me. I would not have to do dishes. My parents have DirecTV. They have internet access. They have a nice spa. I would have a big, comfy bed. So I moved back in with my parents for awhile. I do not remember how long I was living with them, but it seemed like an eternity. I had to be driven everywhere again because it is very hard to drive with a broken collarbone, not to mention three cracked ribs. After a few days, I was able to drive and so I could move back into my own place. What a relief! You never realize what you have until it's gone. That sounds cheesy and is a total cliché but it is so true. I never, ever, **_ever,_** wanted to end up in the St. Helena Hospital and Health Center or their physical therapy place again, so I sold my mountain bike. Before I sold it, I took into the local bike shop for a tune up. While taking my mountain bike there, I was having second thoughts. *I can't get rid of this bike. I love this bike. I can ride it. I'll be Okay.* Then, however, while taking my bicycle out of my shiny new 4Runner, using both arms, I would get jolts of pain that would just knock your socks off. So, I decided, Okay. Enough is enough, and sold the mountain bike.

Whew! That was hard. I did, however, have one bit of solace: I still had my road bicycle. I know what you are thinking. "He can't seriously be thinking about riding his road bike again. Can He?"Well, yes I can, and I was. Don't ask me why or anything sensible like that. My testosterone level was reaching dangerous levels. Fortunately, common sense won and I did not ride my road bicycle, or any bicycle for that matter. I took up golf instead. I had played a lot of golf in high school, but I quit because I could not deal with all the shitheads who thought they were great golfers and had all the nice equipment, but were, in fact, total arrogant jackasses who could not play at all. Fortunately, I was only able to play on Tuesday's, so all the arrogant jackasses were not there.

I don't know if what I played could have been called "golf", but it got me outside and I had fun. In addition, there were not any women out there to make me depressed. What do I mean by that? Thanks to Julie calling the cops on me, I thought I must be so ugly and so disgusting that she feared for her safety. In addition, I thought I must have done something that I had forgotten about and that was worthy of getting the law involved. I thought, *Well, if I do whatever I did again, I might end up in prison.* Also, I thought that I was so ugly, that I must scare and repulse people. As one might imagine, I avoided people, especially women. That made me more depressed and pissed-off. Whenever I saw an attractive female, I would go the other way, hope she did not see me, and would not call the cops. My self-esteem, self-image, and self-confidence were so low it was wearing me down.

There is a song that pretty much said it all in regard to how Julie made feel about my life. The song is by Godsmack and is called "Sick of Life."

Paralyzed. Nothing's getting through to me
Hypnotized from all my surroundings.
I wanna be something I could never be.
I wanna say things that I could never say.
Yeah, I'm gonna do it again!
Sick of my life. I'm tired of everything in my life.
Dragged down. Rubbing my face in the ground.
No time for the undecided
I wanna know why I've felt alone
And I wanna love. Why am I untouchable?
Yeah, I'm gonna do it again!

Sick of my life. I'm tired of everything in my life.
I never wanted to be sick of my life.

I'm tired of everything in my life.

That is pretty much how I felt. It wasn't good. I hate to dwell on shit, and I know that I should "let it go", but when Julie said the things she said to me, acted the way she did, and then called the cops when I did what she said I should do, it just messed with my mind too much. Now, I'm afraid to even look twice at a female, for fear she will call the cops because I must be so repulsive.

I'm not a writer and did not plan on writing a book, it just sort of happened. As a result, I have absolutely no idea how to finish this book. So I'll let someone else do it. I'll let Dido do it. She has a song entitled "Honestly OK" and it will be a good ending to this book.

I just want to feel safe in my own skin,
I just want to be happy again
I just want to feel deep in my own world
But I'm so lonely I don't want even want to be with myself anymore
On a different day, if I was safe in my own skin, then I wouldn't feel so lost and so frightened
But this is today and I'm lost in my own skin
And I'm so lonely I don't even want to be with
myself anymore
I just want to feel safe in my own skin
I just want to feel happy again

My gums still hurt.